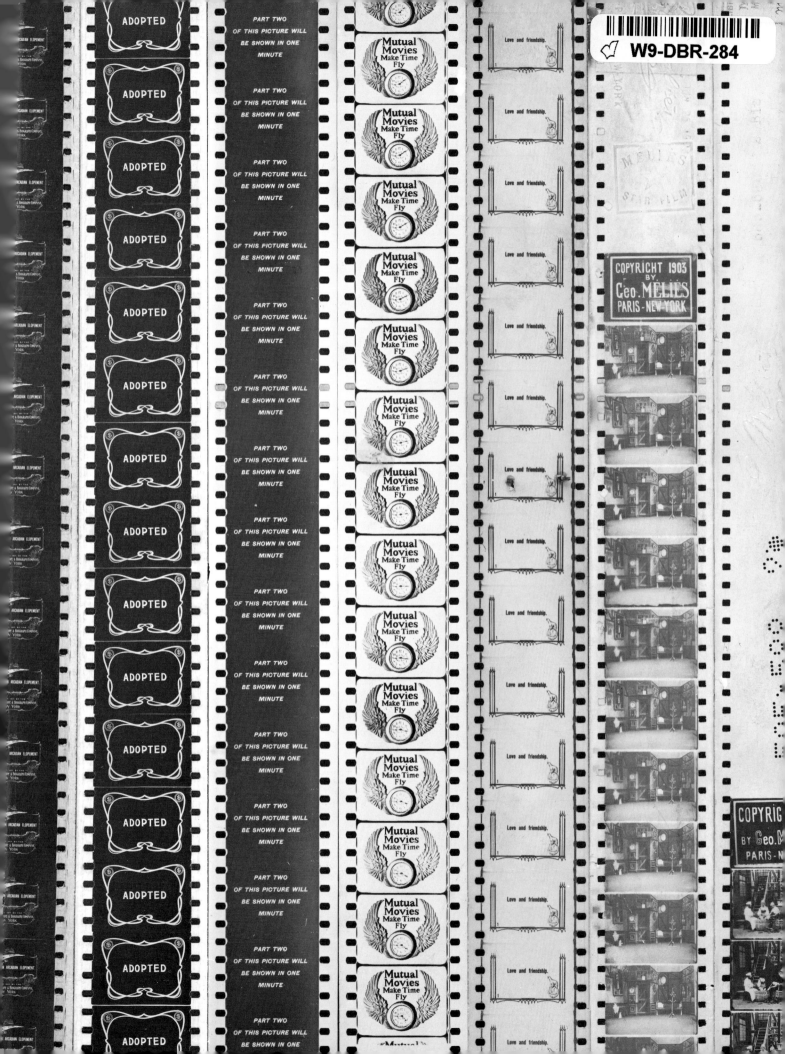

THE FIRST TWENTY YEARS

a segment of film history

by

KEMP R. NIVER

edited by
Bebe Bergsten

ISBN 0-913986-01-1

Locare Research Group

Los Angeles, California

Copyright ©1968 by Kemp R. Niver

Library of Congress Catalog Card Number: 68-58700

Printed by Artisan Press, Los Angeles

Second Edition

INTRODUCTION

This book concerns over one hundred motion pictures selected from the more than 3,000 films restored from the Library of Congress paper print collection. These paper prints, or rolls, were deposited by film producers with the Library of Congress as proof of copyright application prior to ratification in 1912 of a motion picture copyright law. Each film described was selected because, in the author's opinion, it contributed something of value to the progress of communication through the new medium of moving photography.

There are some points, however, that were not a part of the growth of this medium and so were not included in this book. Since they might raise questions, they must be covered in the introduction.

One point is film width. In the majority of instances, the paper rolls sent to the Library of Congress were in 35mm widths, although there certainly was no standardization requirement. In view of this, someone might wonder why the 16mm width was chosen over 35mm for the restored films. There were several reasons for this decision, the foremost of which was consideration of the end use of the films once they were restored. Inasmuch as the films were to be used mainly for study purposes, a size that could be handled simply was decided upon. Another reason, not quite as cogent but nevertheless something to be taken into consideration, was storage space. Last, but definitely not least, was the cost.

Another point that this introduction should explain is the lengths of film. Film 35mm wide is two and one-half times the length, as well as frame area, of 16mm film. If a 35mm roll of paper were 100 feet long, a 16mm reduction would be 40 feet in length. As all of the restoration was done in 16mm, we thought it would be better, except where specifically noted, to use 16mm footage regardless of the width or length of the paper roll. In this way we have standardized all widths of paper in the complete library to 16mm film. In order not to conflict with a catalog of Melies's films published by the British Film Institute, an exception was made. We have used 35mm lengths in discussing his films.

During the course of writing this book, we were delighted that a great deal of new material relating to early film history came to light, and all of it has been added in its position in the scheme of things.

Kemp R. Niver

THE FIRST TWENTY YEARS

Photography, as we know it, had been in existence for approximately half a century before the invention of flexible film made moving pictures feasible. Moving pictures do not move. They are but a series of still photographs in sequence on a strip of light-sensitive flexible film. In order for the eye to perceive and retain the image, each of these pictures must come to a complete stop during projection. This image retention is called persistence of vision, a phenomenon without which motion pictures would be physically impossible.

Consider the quandary in which Thomas A. Edison's patent attorney found himself in 1891 when he was confronted with having to make use of legal terminology in order to describe something that in itself was in conflict with the name given to it. A description was absolutely necessary as Edison was applying for a basic patent on his Kinetograph, his name for a mechanical device that moved a strip of flexible film through its gears and sprockets, stopping approximately forty times a second in order to expose a portion of the film to the light for the purpose of taking a picture at a precise and exact interval. The lawyer who was faced with this task was not aware that his exactness in describing the apparatus would provide the loophole for others to circumvent the patent for a moving picture camera granted to Mr. Edison. In fact, he unwittingly set the playing field for innumerable lawsuits for patent infringement involving some fifty different firms and several hundred persons over a period of nearly twenty years. The litigation ended only when the government strongly suggested putting a stop to it.

Cable Address "Edison, New York."

From the Laboratory
of
Thomas A. Edison.

Orange, N.J. Jan 7/93

Librarian of Congress 506 JAN 9 1894

Dear Sir

Kindly copyright the enclosed title ~~to~~ go with 2 photos following for which please find 50¢.

Very sincerely yours

W.K.L. Dickson

1 Photo

Edison Kinetoscopic Record of a sneeze.

Taken and Copyrighted by W.K.L. Dickson,

Orange New Jersey, January 7th. 1894

Note error in date on application.

Until the motion picture copyright law was enacted about 1912, producers of motion pictures were without copyright protection, so they reached out for an existing law covering still pictures. In 1894, two and a half years after Mr. Edison's patent application for a moving picture camera was filed, his assistant, William K. Laurie Dickson, sent a paper print of a moving picture, EDISON KINETOSCOPIC RECORD OF A SNEEZE, JANUARY 7, 1894, to the Library of Congress, hoping for protection under the still pictures act. Dickson's action in applying for a copyright began a practice that many other producers followed for a period of nearly twenty years. Between 1894 and 1912 in excess of 5,000 paper prints were made from the original negatives and sent from various parts of the world to the Library of Congress for register of copyright where they remained virtually forgotten until 1952 when the Academy of Motion Picture Arts and Sciences started a successful restoration program. By the time restoration began, only 3,000 of these paper rolls remained, and all were converted back into their original state of being motion pictures on flexible film.

Edison Kinetoscopic Record Of A Sneeze

Top sample shows how some paper rolls looked after 50 years of storage, and what needed to be done before the rolls could be restored.

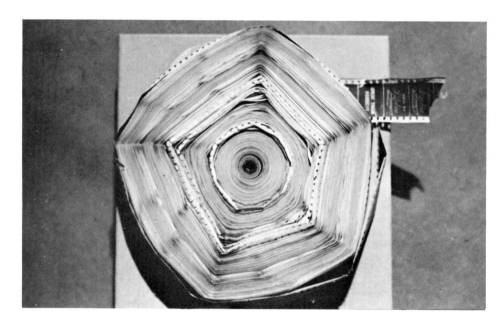

Bottom sample shows the same roll as it looked after restoration.

It is with these particular films that this book is concerned.

During the years of restoration by photography of this collection of paper rolls, it became evident that we had witnessed man's earliest attempt to communicate through the use of motion pictures. As the work continued, we became aware of the existence of various paths the pioneer film-makers had travelled in their eagerness to express themselves, provide entertainment, and make money through this new medium. Of the three thousand motion pictures restored from rolls of paper, only about one hundred were selected for discussion in this book. From time to time, however, other titles from the paper print collection also will be mentioned. We will discuss in chronological order those we have selected and whatever is known about the methods used or the persons who produced these early motion pictures will be included.

At the start of movement in photography, apparently it never occurred to film-makers to use the camera for anything other than to record actual incidents or events, and it was not until man learned how to use a camera as a tool to express himself that motion pictures became an art form. Deciding upon a subject for a motion picture was not much of a task in the years between 1890 and 1896 for the only device in which the film could be viewed limited it to about fifty feet in length, with a running time of approximately one minute. Producers filmed such happenings as sporting events, railroad trains passing by, or children jumping rope. In fact, anything that moved was greeted with amazement by an eager audience. Shortly after motion picture projection became popular in the late 1890s, the novelty of movement began to wear off. Projection attracted a more sophisticated audience who demanded movies that held their interest not on the basis of movement alone but because something was taking place on the screen with which they could identify. Short lengths of raw stock limited movie makers. Nevertheless, with projection of film a new era of film-making began. Few films produced prior to the turn of the century remain today outside the paper print collection that show pre-production preparation or the use of a written script to control the actors or the photography, so it is difficult to pinpoint the exact date when the transition from "instant" movies to planned ones took place. There are, however, approximately one hundred films of less than fifty feet in length restored from paper that indicate pre-production was part of some film-maker's thinking some years before 1900.

Before we start to discuss the three films chosen from this period, the following chronology might be helpful as background material.

August 1891 — Thomas A. Edison applied for patents on Kinetoscope (viewing device) and Kinetograph (photographic device).

T. A. EDISON.
APPARATUS FOR EXHIBITING PHOTOGRAPHS OF MOVING OBJECTS.
No. 493,426.   Patented Mar. 14, 1893.

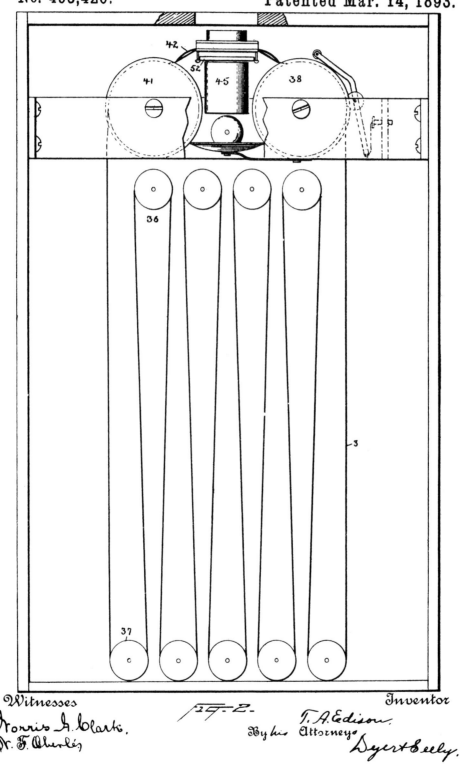

Witnesses   Inventor

Norris S. Clark.   T. A. Edison
N. F. Charles.   By his Attorneys
                                          Dyer & Seely.

T. A. EDISON.
KINETOGRAPHIC CAMERA.

No. 589,168.   Patented Aug. 31, 1897.

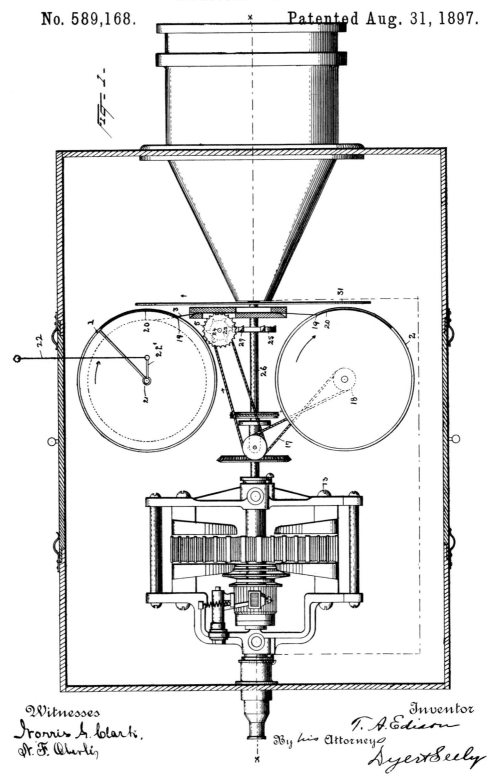

Fig. 1.

Witnesses
Morris S. Clark.
N. F. Clark

Inventor
T. A. Edison
By his Attorneys
Dyer & Seely

ELOPEMENT ON HORSEBACK
STRANGE ADVENTURE OF NEW YORK DRUMMER
LOVE AND WAR

The three motion pictures, ELOPEMENT ON HORSEBACK, STRANGE ADVEN-TURE OF NEW YORK DRUMMER, and LOVE AND WAR, have several things in common. They are among the earliest examples of motion pictures that can be classified as narrative films. All show pre-production thinking, either by use of a script or through rehearsal, and are not news events but planned stories, so short no titles are necessary to indicate the action. One over-all title is sufficient.

For the first film, ELOPEMENT ON HORSEBACK, four complete scenes in only 18 feet were used to tell the story. Some of the problems that a photographer of that era was forced to cope with are clearly evident in this little film. Only high contrast film with an opaque base and very slow exposure rating was used by photographers because of light loss in a peep show. It wasn't until projection of film was possible that the opaque base was no longer needed. There must have been some planning and at least one rehearsal before the camera began cranking. Establishment of exact production date of ELOPEMENT ON HORSEBACK is not possible, but the shape and number of sprocket holes at the edge of the film indicate that it was photographed some months before it was copyrighted by Edison on November 26, 1898.

Above is one frame from scene three of ELOPEMENT ON HORSEBACK. The whole motion picture was less than 20 feet in length.

STRANGE ADVENTURE OF NEW YORK DRUMMER (Edison, copyright June 17, 1899) is one of the earliest examples in the paper print collection of a photographer making use of editing to convey the idea of appearance and disappearance of objects and people.

STRANGE ADVENTURE attempts to show what happened to a travelling salesman who spent the night in a haunted hotel room. Again the number and size of sprocket holes indicate that it was produced at an earlier time than its copyright date. There are very distinct signs of pre-production planning in this motion picture as well as the probability of several rehearsals. The set was constructed, props were placed, and persons or props caused to appear and disappear through the use of stop camera action. Pre-production planning was needed for the effective use of editing to convey a sense of magic, made possible by shooting each scene twice and removing the unwanted film frames. Note the splice marks adjacent to the frameline in photograph below.

Two scenes from STRANGE ADVENTURE OF NEW YORK DRUMMER that show trick photography through editing.

LOVE AND WAR

LOVE AND WAR, a little motion picture made by James H. White in 1899, has the distinction of being one of the first films of its kind ever made. It has five separate scenes, and the camera was moved to a different location for each. Made at the time of the Spanish-American war, its story line was undoubtedly taken from an actual happening. James H. White, employed by Edison at the time, produced the film and copyrighted it on November 28, 1899 in his own name.

The film begins with the hero's departure; scenes of the battle follow.

*Love
And
War*

The young man is wounded, removed from the battlefield, restored to health at a military field hospital, returned to his family — all in a brief 71 feet. The film has no titles to suggest what might be forthcoming. Figure 11 shows that the cameraman was not too sure of the scope of his lens as he not only shot over the top of the walls of the house but the floor also seems to be too small.

In October of 1896, James H. White, photographer, went to work for Edison. He previously had been employed by Holland Brothers and Raff & Gammon, franchise brokers for Kinetoscope parlors. White, with Edwin S. Porter as an assistant, was in charge of the historic evening in April when the novelty, motion picture projection, was introduced at Koster and Bial's Music Hall in New York.

James White left the Edison Company in Orange in 1903 to become manager of an Edison subsidiary, the National Phonograph Company, in Antwerp. His brother, Arthur, who started working for Edison a year before James, remained in the motion picture industry with such firms as Vitagraph, etc. until his death, but after about twenty years in various phases of the film world, James White went on to other things.

Love
And
War
Figure 11

UNCLE JOSH'S NIGHTMARE

UNCLE JOSH'S NIGHTMARE is included with this group of American primitive films as it is another example of the story limitations cumbersome moving picture equipment placed upon the film-maker of that day and how he surmounted those problems. It was made by the Edison company, and the shadows on the rear wall indicate that it was photographed in the "Black Maria" studio. The technique or method of causing the devil and the furniture to appear and disappear was done by editing after the scene was photographed and not in the camera. The film was photographed from a single camera position. The part of Uncle Josh was played by Charles "Daddy" Manley.

Notice editing splice marks in UNCLE JOSH'S NIGHTMARE. The story line of UNCLE JOSH'S NIGHTMARE is practically the same as that of STRANGE ADVENTURE OF NEW YORK DRUMMER, but the sets differ. The 57-foot UNCLE JOSH'S NIGHT-MARE was copyrighted by Edison on March 21, 1900.

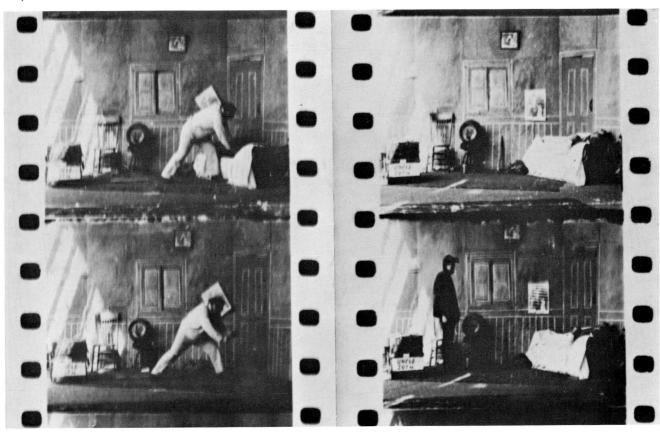

By the time the 20th century began, motion pictures had already been in existence for about ten years, but they didn't become commonplace until motion picture projection began to eliminate the peep show. A myriad of conflicting claims have been made as to early use of a moving picture projection machine. Perhaps the following long quote from the NEW HAVEN MORNING NEWS of December 4, 1896 may help to bring some order out of that chaos:

"When Edison invented the Vitascope, using the principle of the Kinetoscope to throw the moving pictures on a canvas screen, it was thought that the highest degree had been attained in this direction. Mr. Lumiere of Lyons, however, improved on the Vitascope, inventing the Cinematographe, which went a step higher in the art, and now an American, Herman Casler of Canostota, N. Y., has again come to the front, improving on all his predecessors in giving us the Biograph, the most perfect machine yet devised to show moving pictures.

"All three machines have been exhibited in New Haven. The Cinematographe enjoyed a run of eight weeks at the Wonderland, and was seen by thousands. It has now been superseded by the Biograph, which has the additional advantage of showing entirely American views as well as views taken in New Haven. In other cities also it is taking the place of the Cinematographe, and president manager Fynes of the Union Square Theatre in New York has taken out the Cinematographe after a six months run and is negotiating for the Biograph. This means that on the entire Keith circuit the Biograph will be substituted, as well as in other legitimate theatres, and the Cinematographe, like the Vitascope and other less perfect machines, may have to recourse to store shows and nickel in-the-slot devices to stand up. The Biograph is so far superior, both in quality of the views shown and the perfection of their display, that there is really no comparison between it and any of the other machines for the display of motion photography.

"The Biograph is to remain on exhibition at the Wonderland next week, and any one who has seen the Cinematographe can assure himself of the immense superiority of the other by seeing it and comparing it with Mr. Lumiere's invention."

From the foregoing, it is clear that some of the confusion as to who did what arose from the very few months involved. The dates below, taken from press releases of the era, may aid in establishing the chronology of public exhibition of moving picture projection in America:

EDISON KINETOSCOPE (peepshow) exhibited by Holland Brothers at the Grand Central Palace in New York throughout the Fall of 1894, and then toured the country.

EDISON VITASCOPE exhibited for the first time at the Koster & Bial Music Hall in New York City in April of 1896.

LUMIERE CINEMATOGRAPHE first exhibited in America in Keith's Union Square Theatre in New York City in June of 1896.

AMERICAN MUTOSCOPE & BIOGRAPH COMPANY'S BIOGRAPH first public exhibition in Hammerstein's Olympia Theatre in New York City in the Fall of 1896.

It is interesting to note that although the Edison Vitascope was being used at Koster & Bial's Music Hall from April of 1896, by October of the same year it had been replaced by AM&B's Biograph. By making the Biograph projector a part of a vaudeville act and supplying a projectionist, plus a cameraman and a camera to take local views, as one entertainment package that traveled from city to city, the Biograph had been seen in several hundred theatres in America within a very few months.

Some years later an article by J. Austin Fynes appeared in the January 11, 1908 issue of VIEWS AND FILM INDEX. Fynes, an ex-newspaperman, was the manager of Keith's Union Square Theatre, one of America's largest vaudeville houses. His recollections add something to the early days of the moving picture world. Fynes wrote:

"I never saw a more startled audience than that which, on Monday night in June of that eventful year (1896) saw the Lumiere Cinematograph exhibited for the first time in America.

"My advanced advertising had been liberal and quite florid in tone; the house was packed; a fairly strong vaudeville entertainment was half completed when the picture-screen — then an ordinary white sheet — was lowered, and the first motion-photograph was thrown on . . . . They increased the business of that playhouse (Keith's Union Square Theatre) from an average of $4,000 a week to $7,500 a week — and this without Sundays. They brought into the atmosphere of 'vaudeville' a new class of patrons, the most select that had ever visited that style of show . . . . All through that long, hot summer the motion pictures at Keith's held the town enthralled. Packed to its utmost capacity, day after day, the theatre established what I believe to be the highest record of any out-and-out vaudeville theatre in New York City; for its net profits that season figured close to $125,000!

"The phenomenally quick growth of motion picture shows in our American theatres is easy to recall. Within twelve months from the first exhibit, every vaudeville theatre in this land had a picture machine of some sort or another as part of its programme . . . shrewd businessmen soon perceived that here was a new field for a profitable investment. And an innovation which had at first appeared to be ephemeral, rapidly assumed a very sustantial permanency."

Exchange of motion pictures between countries began at once, and, because of this, developments in motion picture techniques in England and France were known and used by American film-makers and vice versa. In fact, the films that have survived show that the techniques of motion picture-making progressed at about the same speed all over the world.

EDISON/PORTER ERA BEGINS

As time goes by and historians research records, additional names of cameramen turn up who, because they were there at the start, could not have helped but make some contribution to the new form of entertainment. For some reason, most of their names have been lost in time, but there is one man whose name has lived because of his contributions to early motion pictures. That man is Edwin S. Porter. If ever there was a business and a man that were instinctively compatible and ready for one another, it was the moving picture business and Porter. He had the mechanical ability to construct a motion picture camera, the knowledge to operate it, the skill to develop film, as well as the creativity to design a production to increase the appeal of the films he made at a period when a new thought in motion pictures was sadly needed.

Just about the time motion picture projection was getting started, Porter left the U.S. Navy and went to work in New York as an electrician for Raff & Gammon, agents for the Edison Kinetoscope and Vitascope viewing device and projector. He helped White to install the projector used on that well-known evening of mid-April to exhibit motion pictures at the Koster & Bial Music Hall. In October of that year, Porter left on a barnstorming tour to exhibit motion pictures in Canada and Central and South America. Porter returned to New York some time in 1897 and went into partnership with W. J. Beadnell to manufacture motion picture cameras and projectors. Fire wiped out their business in 1900.

In 1900 Edwin S. Porter turned his sometime freelance job with Edison into a permanent one when he was put in charge of their glass-enclosed studio at 41 East 21st Street in New York. The Edison company had been making motion pictures for more than six years and had copyrighted some 500 films before Porter went to work there, but the majority were for use in the Kinetoscope or peep show viewing device. The usual subject of these motion pictures was a sporting or news event, or a vaudeville act. Because of the lack of records, it is hard to provide an exact figure, but it is estimated that at least one-third of these 500 films were photographed by roving cameramen, both in the United States and abroad, and sold to the Edison company for distribution.

TERRIBLE TEDDY, THE GRIZZLY KING

A great many film historians seem to believe that Porter was influenced by European motion pictures. This may have been so, but it is more probable that European film-makers stimulated rather than influenced his thinking, for all his moving pictures have a distinctly individual style, while some of them are entirely new in concept. Many motion pictures made outside the United States, as well as many made in America, were never copyrighted by the paper print method and so were lost. But, by looking at the surviving films, it is obvious that the techniques of motion picture-making were well known in this country even before Porter joined Edison in 1900. Actually, techniques in the United States were on a par with those of any other country, even in the beginning of movement in photography.

Porter's capability in making entertainment films soon became evident, and we have chosen five examples of his earliest work. Each shows his ability to use a camera in such a way that it added value and interest to the production.

To make TERRIBLE TEDDY, THE GRIZZLY KING, Porter went outside the studio. TERRIBLE TEDDY could have been made from one camera position, customary in those days, but it seemed to require camera movement. The result was a more interesting film. Teddy Roosevelt, the subject of what may be the first filmed political satire, was the popular vice president of the United States and a rugged outdoorsman. In this 27-foot motion picture, Roosevelt is photographed overacting as he fires a rifle into a tree to drop a housecat at his feet. Teddy dramatically drives a knife in for the kill. All his actions are closely attended by two men wearing placards on their chests that read, "My Press Agent" and "My Photographer." The camera moves back from the scene of carnage, and the actor who plays Teddy Roosevelt majestically mounts his horse. He rides toward the camera followed by his two aides still clutching their identification signs to their chests. TERRIBLE TEDDY was copyrighted by Edison on February 23, 1901.

LOVE BY THE LIGHT OF THE MOON

Edwin S. Porter found that interesting motion pictures could also be made, however, by remaining in the studio and applying camera effects to the production. (Incidentally, the famous "Black Maria" studio constructed by William K. Laurie Dickson for Edison and completed in 1892 fell into disuse and was torn down in 1903.)

Copyrighted by Edison on March 16, 1901, LOVE BY THE LIGHT OF THE MOON is a pleasant, short movie. By bringing animation to the face of the moon through the use of projected slides to supplement the simple story, Porter turned it into a very interesting little film. The 26-foot motion picture begins on a set of a park on a summer evening. There is a fence railing, some foliage, and a park bench, as well as a moon, with a painted face, in the sky. A young couple enter and lean on the railing; they look up at the sky. The moon begins to smile. The young couple continue to embrace and the moon's smile grows wider. When they walk over and sit down on the bench, obscuring the moon's view of them, the smile changes to a disappointed frown. As the picture ends, the young man is fanning the young woman with his straw hat because the moon, like a jack-in-the-box, has left the sky and is peering over their shoulders.

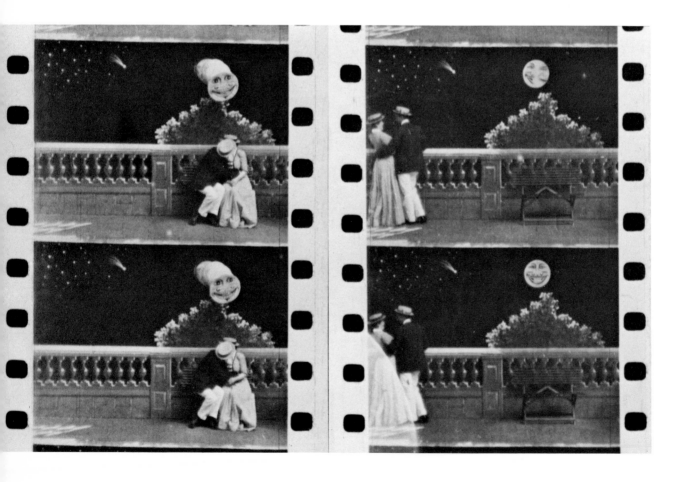

18

CIRCULAR PANORAMA OF ELECTRIC TOWER
PANORAMA OF ESPLANADE BY NIGHT

In 1901 a current event, the Pan-American Exposition in Buffalo, New York, was considered sufficiently important for the Edison company to send Edwin S. Porter there, where he made two documentary films, CIRCULAR PANORAMA OF ELECTRIC TOWER and PANORAMA OF ESPLANADE BY NIGHT. To photograph the first, a 54-foot film, Porter placed his camera high on a building, thus enlarging the scope of his lens. There were too many structures at the fair spread out over too large a territory to be photographed from one position, so in order to encompass all the wonders of the Exposition, Porter constructed a geared camera mount permitting him to turn the camera horizontally in a circle. This is now referred to as "panning," but when the film was copyrighted on August 14, 1901, it was a noteworthy innovation.

Circular Panorama of Electric Tower

When Porter started to photograph PANORAMA OF ESPLANADE BY NIGHT, this technique apparently was not quite enough, as one of the attractions of the Exposition was that it was lighted entirely by electricity. There was no precedent for motion picture photography after dark, so again Porter was presented with a challenge to his skill and imagination. To cope with it, he revamped his motion picture camera to permit him to make a time exposure of each frame of motion picture film. Porter's calculations directed that he expose each of the frames for a minimum of ten seconds. Simple mathematics suggest that most of the night was spent making this 27-foot film. Reputedly the first motion picture ever photographed after dark, PANORAMA OF ESPLANADE BY NIGHT was made September 5, 1901, but not copyrighted by the Edison company until November 11, 1901.

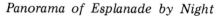

Panorama of Esplanade by Night

MARTYRED PRESIDENTS

That same year, the shooting of President McKinley prompted Edwin S. Porter to make a film with a theme of social significance. It was called MARTYRED PRESIDENTS, and copyrighted by Edison on October 7, 1901. The 20-foot film was a memorial in tableau form to the three American presidents who had been assassinated up to that time. To capitalize on this news event, Porter built a set resembling a monument on which the three martyred presidents (Lincoln, Garfield, and McKinley) were to appear. Porter's method was to photograph life-sized pictures of the three men. He first blocked out the lens visibility with a matte, which, in this instance, was a piece of cardboard with an oval-shaped hole in it. Porter then rephotographed the monument in such a manner that the pictures of Lincoln, Garfield, and McKinley interchanged as the film progressed, with a fade to black between each picture. The last few frames of the motion picture show a symbol of justice, sans eye bandage, holding a tilted scale. Porter made use of this effect again almost five years later in a far more elaborate production, THE KLEPTOMANIAC, also a picture with a theme of social significance.

UNCLE JOSH AT THE MOVING PICTURE SHOW

Copyrighted by Thomas A. Edison on January 27, 1902, UNCLE JOSH AT THE MOVING PICTURE SHOW is another excellent example of how early in his film-making career Porter was able to incorporate all manner of camera uses into a film in order to enhance the story. In the 65 years that have elapsed since the era under discussion, two films have become almost synonomous with the name Edwin S. Porter. They are LIFE OF AN AMERICAN FIREMAN, copyrighted January 21, 1903, and THE GREAT TRAIN ROBBERY, copyrighted December 1, 1903. Each in its own way is a milestone, yet UNCLE JOSH made nearly a year earlier, contains the same techniques that were considered such innovations in LIFE OF AN AMERICAN FIREMAN and THE GREAT TRAIN ROBBERY.

The plot of UNCLE JOSH AT THE MOVING PICTURE SHOW is a simple one. It concerns a country bumpkin who becomes so overwhelmed by watching his first motion picture from a stage box that he tears down the screen in his enthusiasm to help the heroine of one of the films.

UNCLE JOSH is a particularly intriguing motion picture, for Porter used live action combined with previously photographed film projected on a screen, to which he added double exposure and matte shots. Some of these effects were achieved by the use of an optical printer that had been manufactured on the Edison premises. Each segment of pre-photographed film was preceded by a specially designed title, unusual for that day. The three films Porter used are BLACK DIAMOND EXPRESS, copyrighted December 12, 1896,

Uncle Josh at the Moving Picture Show

PARISIAN DANCE, copyrighted January 15, 1897, and COUNTRY COUPLE, which probably was photographed specifically for UNCLE JOSH, as no copyright date exists. BLACK DIAMOND EXPRESS and PARISIAN DANCE were distributed by Edison some years before Porter arrived there and could very well be all that remains of some of their earliest films.

Uncle Josh
At The
Moving
Picture
Show

THE TWENTIETH CENTURY TRAMP

One of the enigmas that confronts researchers on early motion pictures is the lack of records to definitely establish date of an occurrence. The next film, THE TWENTIETH CENTURY TRAMP, bears the same copyright date as UNCLE JOSH, but it is hard to say when it actually was made. The combination of pan, double exposure, and matte shot represents one of the earliest uses of this effect that we were able to find among the restored paper prints. It is still another example of Porter's continuing search for various ways to make motion pictures entertaining. Only 38 feet long, THE TWENTIETH CENTURY TRAMP is a motion picture of a man riding a bicycle suspended beneath an airship over a film of a 180° pan of the New York skyline. The identical panoramic view appears in DREAM OF A RAREBIT FIEND, a film that attracted great attention when it was released in 1906, four years later.

THE TWENTIETH CENTURY TRAMP is subtitled HAPPY HOOLIGAN AND HIS AIRSHIP. In the few years preceding Edwin S. Porter's association with the Edison firm, someone hit upon the idea of making a series of narrative-type films based on a popular cartoon character named Happy Hooligan, a creation of famed illustrator, Frederick Burr Opper. J. Stuart Blackton, later one of the founders of the Vitagraph, often acted the part of Happy Hooligan in motion pictures.

FUN IN A BAKERY SHOP

Edwin S. Porter was confronted with a dilemma when he turned to the stage for new subjects for motion pictures. The usual stage act greatly exceeded the running time of the piece of negative available to the cameraman of that day. Nevertheless, Porter succeeded in condensing a humorous vaudeville act into a film that ran less than one minute. The motion picture, called FUN IN A BAKERY SHOP, was copyrighted by Edison on April 3, 1902. Thirty-seven feet long, the film shows a baker/sculptor beset by co-workers and a rat, as he rapidly sculpts loaves of clay into faces of famous individuals. To insure the smooth flow of the motion picture, Porter stopped the camera at regular intervals, starting it again only when the sculptor's hands had returned to the same position in his modeling clay. Today, to make a full production cartoon, the same method of delay of camera is used.

When we examined the paper print of FUN IN A BAKERY SHOP, it was discovered that Porter also edited out frames from the negative. He did this to add further smoothness to the motion picture, as well as to eliminate jump cuts caused by starting and stopping the camera.

JACK AND THE BEANSTALK

Edwin S. Porter, after two years of making motion pictures in various ways, now undertook his most ambitious and also his longest film up to that time. It was the 250-foot film, JACK AND THE BEANSTALK, copyrighted by Edison on June 20, 1902. JACK AND THE BEANSTALK is a well-known fairy tale and was a current stage play. The film format resembles the popular fantasy films of the type that brought the French film-maker, Georges Melies, great recognition.

Jack and the Beanstalk

When Porter made JACK AND THE BEANSTALK, he really outdid himself. The sets were extremely impressive, for they showed considerable ingenuity in their design. The sets consisted of a waterfall that moved, a waterwheel that turned, doors and windows that actually opened and closed. Throughout the film, Porter used the possibilities of a moving picture camera in a new way through the spectacular use of dissolves between scenes, stop camera action to allow people to appear and disappear, and the use of lantern slides as a projector of thought within a moving picture production. When the film was released in 1902, a black and white print cost $93.75, while a hand-colored print came to $233.75.

The only other production of this magnitude made by Edwin S. Porter that was restored from paper prints was a film called PARSIFAL, in eight scenes, based on an opera. PARSIFAL will be discussed in detail in its proper chronological place.

*Jack
And
The
Beanstalk*

GRANDPA'S READING GLASS

On October 3, 1902, Edison's chief competitor, the American Mutoscope & Biograph Company, then located at 841 Broadway in New York City, copyrighted a 34-foot film called GRANDPA'S READING GLASS that is evidence that films with pre-production thinking, combined with highly developed editing and camera techniques were being produced by firms other than Edison in those early years.

The motion picture begins by showing some children grouped about an old gentleman who is reading with a magnifying glass. The children borrow the magnifying glass from him to look at various objects. Each time they do so, the object is shown in extreme closeup from the point of view of the person holding the glass. This was a most unusual camera technique for 1902, and no earlier example exists in the paper print collection.

To emphasize the impression of point of view, Robert K. Bonine, the photographer, used a round matte, a piece of black cardboard in which a circular hole had been cut.

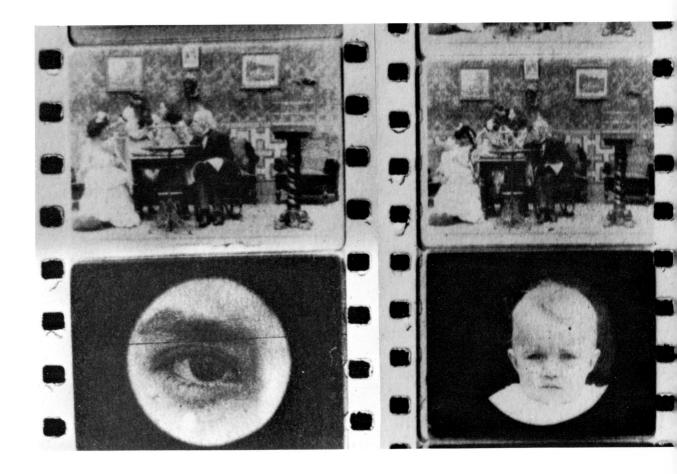

LIFE OF AN AMERICAN FIREMAN

Toward the end of 1902, Edwin S. Porter planned another motion picture project. He began by writing a story in seven scenes to enable him to use previously photographed film which he supplemented by shooting several new scenes to add to its excitement. He called his moving picture LIFE OF AN AMERICAN FIREMAN. The completed film was 169 feet long, and was copyrighted by Edison on January 21, 1903.

The film follows a story line of a woman and child trapped in a burning building who are saved by the heroism and skill of the fire department, and the expert use of its equipment. In every one of the several Porter films already mentioned, there has been one or more example of his ability to enhance a story through the use of special effects, whether it was a matte shot, double exposure, stop action, or some other new method of special photographic effect.

Porter began LIFE OF AN AMERICAN FIREMAN by showing the principals in the story in the same frame of the film. This was accomplished by double exposure. A closeup of a hand activating a fire alarm box starts the action of the film. In his original scenario of LIFE OF AN AMERICAN FIREMAN, Porter mentions that there is to be a dissolve between each of the seven scenes. Careful examination of the paper prints made for copyright purposes clearly shows two separate sets of sprocket holes, indicating that Porter joined together scenes by a dissolve made in a machine, or printer, by overlapping previously photographed film with newly photographed film. Somewhere in each of the interior scenes, a placard bearing the Thomas A. Edison copyright notice appears.

THE INN WHERE NO MAN RESTS

At the close of 1895, after a public exhibition of motion pictures in France, Georges Melies persuaded an inventor by the name of Georges Demeny to sell him a motion picture camera. At that time Melies was a successful professional magician and owner of the Robert-Houdin theatre in Paris.

Catalogs show that in the succeeding fifteen years, Melies made over 1,500 films. Few exist today, but from those that remain it is evident that his usual format for a motion picture was similiar to a magician's vaudeville act. Occasionally, however, Melies made a film based on a current event or one that followed a previously written story. Such a film is THE INN WHERE NO MAN RESTS, copyrighted on June 25, 1903. The 147-foot film consists of a series of scenes of an inebriated guest at an inn, and his many misadventures are shown in Melies's best manner of fantasy.

A SPIRITUALIST PHOTOGRAPHER

When Melies made A SPIRITUALIST PHOTOGRAPHER, he reverted to his usual style of a motion picture depicting a magician at work. In the 85-foot film, copyrighted July 6, 1903, Melies causes a woman to appear and disappear, as if she were a painting in a frame. Later in the film, the woman comes to life and walks toward the camera.

A SPIRITUALIST PHOTOGRAPHER begins with Melies holding a sign lettered in both French and English that reads, "Spiritualistic Photo. Dissolving Effect. Obtained Without Black Background. Great Novelty," which it certainly was. In order to accomplish this photographic trick of double exposure, a black background generally was used by those who knew how, but Melies achieved the same effect by shooting each scene twice — once with the object and once without it — and then editing the two pieces of film together at the point desired. Melies made use of this editing technique for both THE INN WHERE NO MAN RESTS and A SPIRITUALIST PHOTOGRAPHER. All of his films show a great deal of pre-production work and precise timing, and there were many rehearsals before a motion picture actually was photographed.

UNCLE TOM'S CABIN

Mr. J. Austin Fynes, manager of B.T. Keith's Union Square Theatre in New York, said in an article he wrote for the January 1908 VIEWS AND FILM INDEX, "'Novelty' was then as now the constant cry — both from patrons, and from managers." Man probably never developed a field of endeavor that so continually taxed his imagination in order to survive as the motion picture business. The producer was always in a sink-or-swim situation. His next production had to exceed the last one, and this was true right from the start. We have already said that if there was a man and a business that were made for each other, it was Edwin S. Porter and the motion picture business. For one thing, he learned more quickly than any other American film-maker of his time how to take a simple story and increase its entertainment value through the use of a new tool, the motion picture camera. In an effort to bring novelty to motion pictures, Porter resorted to the stage on more than one occasion as a source of inspiration. In 1903, he took one of America's most popular and influential stage productions, UNCLE TOM'S CABIN, and turned it into an entertaining film.

Scenes From Uncle Tom's Cabin

Porter followed the stage play closely, but he made opportunities throughout the film to show how motion pictures could provide greater scope for dramatizing a story or play than the stage could offer. For instance, when Little Eva and Uncle Tom are dying, Porter did not overlook the chance to again use a camera trick, double exposure, to create the impression that descending angels were going to carry the principals off to their reward. Porter also made use of varied optical effects to increase the impact of their death scenes.

As a substitute for the customary play prologue, Porter thought up titles to precede each act of the play and set the scene to follow. No earlier use of titles between scenes was found in the paper print collection.

For his motion picture, Porter also added a race between two paddle-wheel steamers, the "Natchez" and the "Robert E. Lee," using miniature ships, floating on a to-scale Mississippi River, complete with a devastating thunderstorm and lightning. To top off this contribution, Porter caused the "Robert E. Lee" to blow up right before the eyes of the interested spectators.

A further example of Porter's inventiveness occurred in UNCLE TOM'S CABIN, when he constructed what appeared to be a river that moved from stage left to right for the Liza-crossing-the-ice scene. For this, Porter converted the waterfall from his earlier motion picture, JACK AND THE BEANSTALK, into a river by turning it sideways. For one scene, Porter ingeniously transformed a daytime set into an evening one by painting windows to look as if they were lighted, adding painted shadows where needed, as if they were caused by the moon he hung on the backdrop. To further substantiate that the scene was taking place at night, Porter also made cut-outs of houses with lighted windows and placed them on the horizon.

Painted slides depicting the end of the Civil War, with scenes such as a slave kneeling at the feet of Abraham Lincoln, Robert E. Lee and General Grant shaking hands, etc., were incorporated into the finale of Porter's magnificent motion picture.

The film was made up of 14 scenes of varying lengths and totalled 507 feet, something of a record for 1903. Incidentally, Uncle Tom was played in blackface, but there were some genuine Negroes among the cast. UNCLE TOM'S CABIN was copyrighted by Edison on July 30, 1903.

A SEARCH FOR EVIDENCE

   Biograph records provided the clue to the cameraman of A SEARCH FOR EVIDENCE. It was George W. "Billy" Bitzer, AM&B's main cameraman, who made a great many other films for them during his nearly two decades there.

   The story line of this dramatic little 85-foot motion picture is built around a suspicious wife who is accompanied by a detective as they search a series of hotel rooms seeking her husband. For each scene the director, Wallace McCutcheon, establishes the hotel room door, and reveals what is happening in the room from the probing wife's point of view through a keyhole-shaped matte. The drama of actually finding the guilty husband and his paramour is accentuated through the device of placing the camera inside the room to show the detective crashing through the door from the other side. This camera placement allowed McCutcheon to depict the excitement of four persons, rather than just two.

   Remember that A SEARCH FOR EVIDENCE was made in 1903, yet these early filmmakers had already discovered the formula for delayed suspense. McCutcheon was aware of parallel action and had learned that by moving a camera he could give the viewer what he thought necessary to hold his interest and to increase impact.

   The "other woman" in A SEARCH FOR EVIDENCE was played by Kathryn Osterman, a New York vaudeville headliner. The film, copyrighted on August 3, 1903, was produced at AM&B's new studio location at 11 East 14th Street, New York City, which remained their headquarters for about ten years.

GAY SHOE CLERK
THE DUDE AND THE BURGLARS

Two short films made on approximately the same day in August of 1903 by competitive companies show that their makers were even then aware that the use of a motion picture camera could greatly increase the impact of a vaudeville show on an audience.

The first, GAY SHOE CLERK, involves a flirtatious shoe clerk, an attractive young lady, and her obese chaperone who is armed with an umbrella. By use of camera movement, in this instance to a tight closeup of the young lady's ankle, Edwin S. Porter made it possible for all members of the moving picture audience to participate in the fun of seeing the young woman's ankle, not just the select few seated in the front rows of the theatre had it been a live performance. GAY SHOE CLERK was copyrighted by Edison on August 12, 1903, and was 28 feet long.

Gay Shoe Clerk

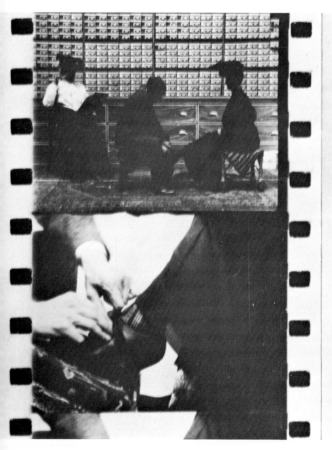 

In the second film, THE DUDE AND THE BURGLARS, which was copyrighted by American Mutoscope & Biograph on August 13, 1903, the director/cameraman had the actors play their parts on a line paralleling the camera, entering and leaving either stage left or right. This technique was necessary as the lenses used in early motion picture photography had a very short depth of focus, limiting the range of movement back and forth in front of a camera. Even with the limitation the mechanical problem placed on the action of the actors, the film audience could see this sophisticated comedy better than most of the members of the stage audience. THE DUDE AND THE BURGLARS was 23 feet long.

The Dude and The Burglars

THE KINGDOM OF THE FAIRIES

By 1903 Georges Melies had been a film-maker in France for nearly ten years. With few exceptions, such as the DREYFUS COURT MARTIAL (1899 in 10 scenes), CINDERELLA (1899 in 20 scenes), the Paris Exposition (1900 newsreel), and A TRIP TO THE MOON (1902 in 30 scenes), none of his several hundred productions was much over 65 feet in length. Then, in 1903, he made a film that was 1,080 feet long, THE KINGDOM OF THE FAIRIES.

All of his pictures were filmed in sections that Melies called tableaux. These tableaux generally were joined together by an in-the-camera dissolve, although the paper prints of his films show that he could also make dissolves in a machine printer. In addition to Melies's ability as a magician, he was a talented and experienced scenic artist. His sets and backdrops attest to his knowledge of artistic perspective and architectural construction, something that few, if any, of his contemporaries shared.

THE KINGDOM OF THE FAIRIES, a motion picture consisting of 32 scenes, is considered to be a more important production than his world-famous A TRIP TO THE MOON. In THE KINGDOM OF THE FAIRIES, Melies employed just about every method of photographic special effect that he knew. There were fades, dissolves, cartoons, stop motion, sliding sets that divide, shooting through fish tanks for an underwater effect, and tabletop miniatures, as well as projected slides, combined with live action. THE KINGDOM OF THE FAIRIES is one of the best, as well as one of three longest, films Melies ever produced. He copyrighted it on September 3, 1903.

The Kingdom of the Fairies

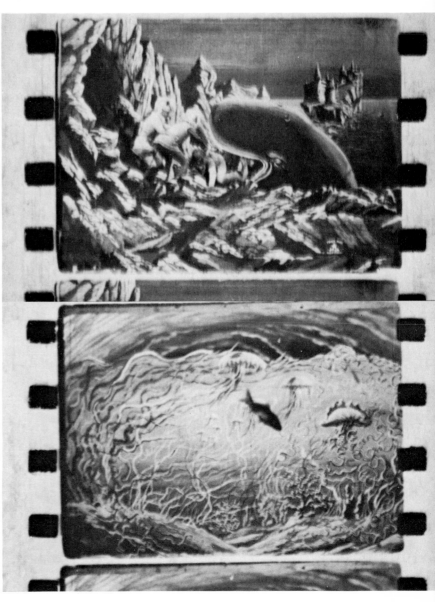

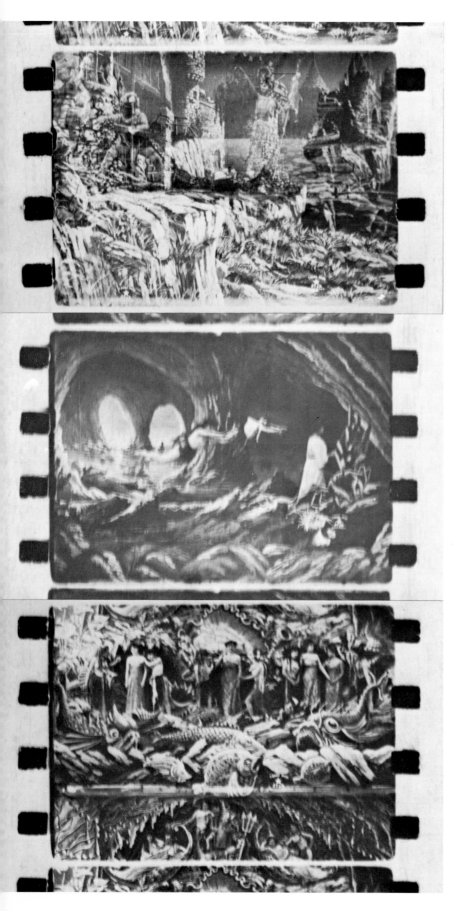

A ROMANCE OF THE RAIL

When the paper prints were restored, a few advertising films turned up, one phase of motion picture-making about which little has been written, even though as far back as 1897 motion picture producers were urging advertisers to use films as another means of selling their products. An excerpt from the Edison catalog of 1897 proclaims, "Special subjects taken for advertising purposes, illustrating songs, etc., for exclusive use of customers. Full particulars as to prices, terms, etc., furnished on application".

Edwin S. Porter made A ROMANCE OF THE RAIL for the Lackawanna Railroad in 1903, and the film was copyrighted by Edison on October 3rd of that year. The plot of this motion picture originated as an advertising scheme in the active imagination of Wendell P. Colton, a Lackawanna employee, who felt he could use this new form of communication as a means to combat the bad impression dirt, soot, and cinders left with railroad passengers of the era.

Colton enlisted the aid of the Edison company, and he and Porter put together a humorous motion picture, featuring the Lackawanna's imaginary character, Phoebe Snow, a traveler who was always attired in immaculate white. To take the part of Phoebe in the film, Colton hired a photographer's model, Marie Murray. The motion picture begins by showing Phoebe Snow seated on a station platform. A man in a white linen suit joins her, and they board the train together. The remainder of the film shows their trip, as well as their marriage en route. Most of the 108-foot motion picture was photographed from a flatcar following the observation platform, where the principals could be seen enjoying the sights, something no railroad passenger of that day would have been brave enough to try dressed conventionally, let alone attired in pure white.

The last scene in the film shows two tramps clad in evening clothes as they crawl out from under the rods of the Lackawanna train. They haughtily refuse the services of a porter, as apparently everyone knew that even tramps didn't need dusting if they rode the Lackawanna.

The contacts that Porter made with the Lackawanna R.R. officials while working on A ROMANCE OF THE RAIL greatly diminished his production problems when he produced THE GREAT TRAIN ROBBERY, perhaps his best remembered film, just two months later.

A Romance of the Rail

THE MAGIC LANTERN

Some time during the year 1902, Georges Melies decided to dispatch his brother, Gaston, from France to America to open a film agency for the distribution in the United States of the Star brand motion pictures that already had won for him a worldwide audience. In announcing the new agency, Melies referred to himself as the originator of motion pictures "made from artificially arranged scenes." THE INN WHERE NO MAN RESTS and THE KINGDOM OF THE FAIRIES, already discussed, certainly bear out his statement. Both were among his most elaborate and outstanding productions.

A SPIRITUALIST PHOTOG-RAPHER, also previously described, and THE MAGIC LANTERN are, however, standard Melies's productions of the type on which his reputation as a motion picture-maker was founded.

The setting for THE MAGIC LAN-TERN is a toy shop where the toys come to life. They dance, juggle, and perform acts of magic, the most unusual of which was the projection of moving images through a magic lantern onto a back wall of a set previously prepared for this purpose.

Melies achieved this trick by matte shots and double exposure. He then edited the surplus frames out of the original negative to facilitate smoothness of action during projection of the finished film. All of the dancers who appeared in the tableaux were professionals from the nearby Folies Bergere. THE MAGIC LANTERN, 315 feet long, was copyrighted by Melies on December 9, 1903.

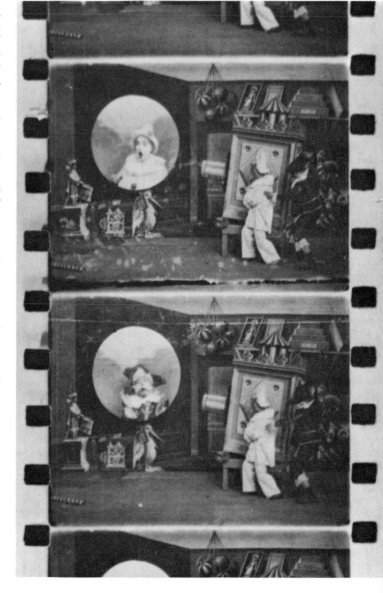

Notice editing splice marks on frame line.

OTHER FOREIGN FILMS

Almost from the very beginning, motion pictures were destined to become an international method of communication. It has been said many times that had Thomas A. Edison troubled to patent his Kinetoscope and Kinetograph in Europe and Great Britain, motion pictures would have been confined to peep show boxes, but this hardly seems likely, for film projection on the screen was inevitable. Magic lantern slide projection had been known for over a hundred years as a visual education aid as well as an entertainment medium. In fact, the flexible film that made moving pictures possible was invented to replace the easily broken glass slides used for magic lanterns.

In mid-1903, the American Mutoscope & Biograph Company of New York set up reciprocal film exchanges with the British producers Warwick Trading Company, Charles Urban Trading Co., Hepworth & Company, and Robert W. Paul, as well as L. Gaumont & Company of London and Paris, and Melies in Paris. A sales feature was that the films were available with sprocket holes to fit American projectors.

Early in film-making history, American film widths and sprocket hole dimensions were accepted and adopted as standard by both the British and the French, thereby extending the economic life of a film by enlarging its market domestically and abroad. American Mutoscope made paper prints of the films they imported, copyrighting and distributing them under the AM&B label, and this is the sole reason that it is possible for us to see many of these foreign films today.

THE PICKPOCKET
HOW THE OLD WOMAN CAUGHT THE OMNIBUS

Again, in order of U.S. copyright date, we would like to talk about two British films: THE PICKPOCKET (produced by Gaumont; copyrighted by AM&B on December 10, 1903), and HOW THE OLD WOMAN CAUGHT THE OMNIBUS (produced by Hepworth and copyrighted by AM&B on December 19, 1903). Both had already been exhibited in England. The AM&B handbills of the day advertise that the British and French motion pictures distributed by them were chosen especially because of the great success they had enjoyed abroad.

The general definition of a "chase" motion picture is a film that begins with one person fleeing from another, with the number of pursuers increasing as the film progresses. That description fits THE PICKPOCKET. The opening scene of the motion picture is of a pickpocket removing a man's watch and chain, while contents of a store window hold the man's interest.

The Pickpocket

When the pickpocket is discovered, he starts to run. He is pursued by police and more police, as well as more and more bystanders. Eventually, he is captured in a lumberyard by the police, but not before a great deal of London is seen by all.

THE PICKPOCKET is 129 feet long and is made up from scenes photographed from at least ten different camera positions. It was directed by Alfred Collins, a former stage director, who worked at Gaumont's London studio.

HOW THE OLD WOMAN CAUGHT THE OMNIBUS is a 69-foot comedy of a ridiculous old woman (obviously played by a man) burdened with a large, over-full box, who makes several unsuccessful attempts to board a horse-drawn, double-decker omnibus. To add to the comical situation, the operator ran the camera backwards, and, on two occasions, dummies were substituted for her falls after the camera was stopped.

How The Old Woman Caught The Omnibus

THE STORY THE BIOGRAPH TOLD

To supply the popular demand for flip cards or one-minute Mutoscope dramas, the American Mutoscope & Biograph Company employed several cameramen, each of whom made some contribution to the technique of motion picture-making. On January 8, 1904, AM&B copyrighted a 117-foot comedy called THE STORY THE BIOGRAPH TOLD, made for them by cameraman A. E. Weed. The plot is of a flirtatious married businessman and his attractive secretary who were photographed by the office boy during the business day. That evening in a theatre his wife sees the office activities of her philandering husband and secretary on the screen.

To let the audience know that the businessman was telephoning to his wife at home, A. E. Weed double exposed a section of the film so that husband, secretary, and wife all appear on the screen together. In order to provide the illusion that his wife is seeing the motion picture, Mr. Weed turned the camera around, had the same scene re-enacted, which changed the point of view of the motion picture audience to that of the office boy, or camera position.

There is certainly nothing unusual about the plot of THE STORY THE BIOGRAPH TOLD, but A. E. Weed's approach to film-making was original for the time and a very definite departure from the type of one-camera-position motion pictures offered to 1904 audiences. The motion picture camera in the film operated by the office boy is a Moy-Basty of British manufacture, not the Biograph camera that was used to make the entire picture.

The Story The Biograph Told

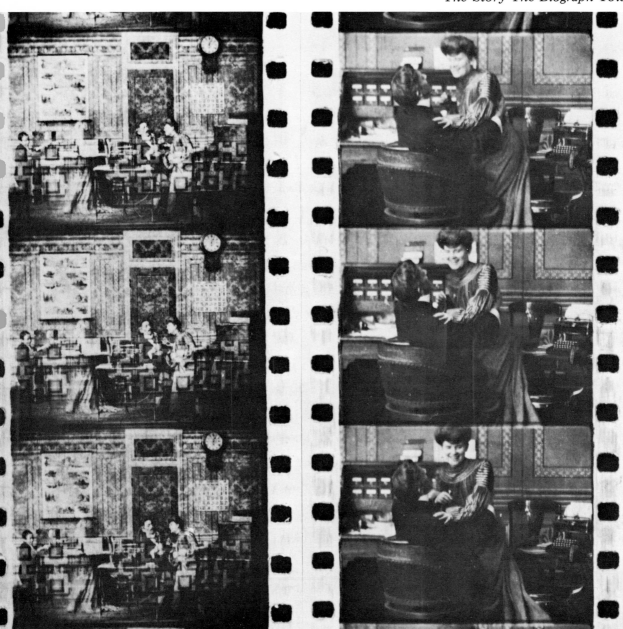

50

THE CLOCK MAKER'S DREAM

THE CLOCK MAKER'S DREAM is a 170-foot film of pure fantasy photographed from a single camera position. Copyrighted by Melies on February 23, 1904, it follows the story line of a clock maker who falls asleep and dreams that his clocks dissolve into pretty girls who dance about him or form attractive tableaux. The picture ends as he awakens and finds himself still in his little clock shop, with everything as it was in the first scene.

THE COOK IN TROUBLE

For the 275-foot THE COOK IN TROUBLE, Melies built a set resembling a large commercial kitchen, where he had a group of circus acrobats costumed as devils harass the cook throughout the film. In THE CLOCK MAKER'S DREAM, people were transformed into clocks and back again by the use of in-the-camera dissolves, but Melies used stop motion editing technique to make the devils in THE COOK IN TROUBLE appear and disappear. Both of these films are longer and more lavish than his standard 65-foot films of earlier years, although they follow the same format. THE COOK IN TROUBLE was copyrighted May 9, 1904.

THE MERMAID

One of the most outstanding and delightful films, both in application of special effects as well as in the use of live actors, that Georges Melies made over the years is the 233-foot THE MERMAID, copyrighted on May 18, 1904. The picture opens in what resembles a living room. Melies, through adroit and expert use of his camera, takes the audience into an undersea grotto constructed in a fish tank. The camera moves in to the opening of the grotto where live fish can be seen swimming around a mermaid that Melies dissolves into the scene. To create the effect of going through many caverns, Melies moved the miniature split set on a specially built inclined track toward the camera, a sort of dolly shot in reverse. All of the underwater scenes were photographed through a fish tank to convey the idea that they were actually photographed under water.

THE CHILD STEALERS

Throughout Melies's 17-year-career as a film-maker, he adhered to the concept of motion pictures based on fantasy, while in England, right from the start, the approach was toward realistic films, with a preponderance of sordid detail. American film-makers of 1904 often made use of newspaper stories of current events as scenarios, usually with little thought of conveying a message. By contrast, the British film-makers pointed out existing social evils by producing documentary/dramas, of which the following are three examples. All were released by L. Gaumont & Company, a pioneer movie-maker that produced films both in France and England.

The first, called THE CHILD STEALERS, released in the United States by AM&B and copyrighted by them on June 9, 1904, is 170 feet in length. The film follows the title and could have been intended as a warning to theatregoers about what might happen to unattended children. During the film, three children are stolen by gypsies under different circumstances, and then taught to beg. The film ends when a mother recognizes her child and summons the police. There is a chase, the gypsies are caught, and all the kidnapped children restored to their parents. The film was photographed outdoors on city streets.

RAID ON A COINER'S DEN
THE EVICTION

RAID ON A COINER'S DEN and THE EVICTION were imported by AM&B and were copyrighted by them on June 23, 1904. Both films begin with a full-frame closeup. At right is the first scene from RAID ON A COINER'S DEN, showing a closeup of a British police pistol, a pair of handcuffs and three pairs of hands.

Raid On A Coiner's Den

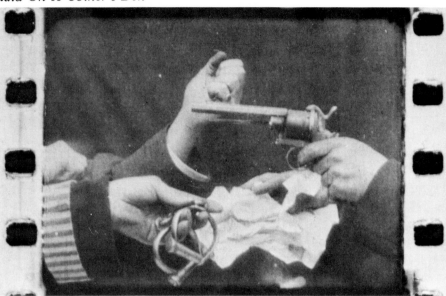

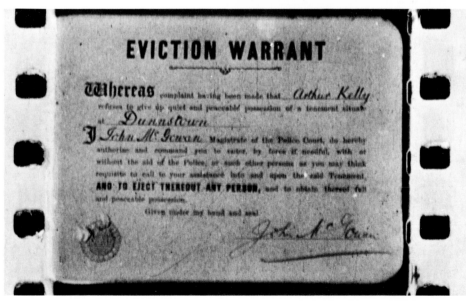

The second film, THE EVICTION, starts out with a full-frame closeup of an eviction warrant.

The Eviction

RAID ON A COINER'S DEN is a 182-foot film in several scenes that show the coiners, or counterfeiters, at work, the police surveillance, detection, the chase, and final apprehension of criminals. There is no doubt that the film is a sober attempt at realism, but in the instance of THE EVICTION, an 84-foot film, there is some doubt in the viewer's mind whether it is intended as a drama or as a comedy. For the length of the film, the police try hard to evict some tenants, who perform many counter actions to thwart them and make them look ridiculous.

Raid On A Coiner's Den

At the finish of RAID ON A COINER'S DEN, there is no question that the police have caught the criminals and brought them to justice, but in THE EVICTION, it is not clear who won. The directors of both films moved the camera a number of times to aid in expressing their ideas. THE EVICTION was directed by Alfred Collins, who may also have directed RAID ON A COINER'S DEN, as both films have the same directorial style, and an examination of the paper prints shows that both were photographed by the identical camera.

The Eviction

FORM NO. 324   BULLETIN No. 28, Aug 15, 1904

"PERSONAL"

THE GREAT COMEDY-HIT CHASE FILM

HELD FOR A RUN AT
KEITH'S UNION SQUARE THEATRE, NEW YORK

Cheers and Laughs from Start to Finish

PERSONAL--Young French gentleman, recently arrived in this country, desires to meet handsome American girl; object matrimony. Will be at Grant's Tomb at 10 this morning, wearing boutonniere of violets.

Alphonse, after inserting this advertisement in the Herald, hies himself in his best apparel to Grant's Tomb, Riverside Drive, New York City, there to meet a fair and financially favored American girl if one shows up. He arrives a little ahead of time, but not too early for an ambitious widow, who, with her small daughter, is parading the beat on the lookout for the Frenchman.

Alphonse sees her first however and nimbly sidesteps, only to be confronted by another fair creature. To her he makes his best obeisance, but has hardly time to introduce himself when another girl claims his attention. In an instant they are on him from all sides. No matter which way he attempts to dodge he is confronted by a determined female. Before he realizes what he is up against he is in the midst of a crowd of husky American girls, in danger of being torn limb from limb. In frantic fear he breaks through the line and starts away on a dead run.

In the next scene we see the desperate man leaving Grant's Tomb in the distance at a 10-second clip, with a cloud of flying petticoats in close pursuit. The chase then developes through successive scenes, each one screamingly funny, and there is always the little fat short-breathed woman who gets left and finishes a bad last.

Across country the chase goes. At one time down a steep embankment, where several of the girls slip and "bump the bumps." The professor in the orchestra plays a solo on the bass drum when this happens, and the audience shouts with laughter. In one of the successive scenes the fat girl gets stuck in a rail fence, in another she almost falls off a plank across a stream. A neat little lady with white stockings also attracts attention as she lifts her fluffy skirts and chases the Frenchman.

Human endurance has a limit, and the Frenchman at last gives out. Breathless and exhausted he takes refuge in a clump of bushes. But fate has overtaken him. One fleet-footed Diana discovers him, and drawing a revolver from her shopping bag she holds him up and claims him for her own. There is nothing for the poor fellow to do but to yield gracefully. The other girls come straggling in, but realizing that the game has been bagged, they extend their congratulations. The whole troup then starts off for the nearest Justice of the Peace.

No film produced up to this time has had the success of "PERSONAL." It has run longer in the Keith houses than any other film of any make has ever run, and it is booked for a return over the entire circuit. It makes the moving picture turn the headliner of a programme.

"Personal," like "The Escaped Lunatic," "Kit Carson," "Out in the Streets," "The Moonshiners" and other great productions of our own manufacture, is restricted to our own use and not for sale. We are the only concern in America prepared to supply an exclusive service.

Produced and Controlled Exclusively by the

American Mutoscope & Biograph Company,

11 EAST 14th STREET, NEW YORK CITY.

PERSONAL

It is evident from a study of the restored paper prints that by 1904 enough time had elapsed for each of the film-making countries of the world to begin producing motion pictures that were individual in style. The French seemed to enjoy producing fantasies that actually were filmed stage productions. British motion pictures were of a more literal and realistic nature, usually based on actual happenings. In the United States, another definite type of motion picture was starting to emerge. It became known as the "chase," and so great was its success, that chase films soon were being produced in every country in the world, as they still are today, in every genre of film, be it drama, comedy, or suspense.

PERSONAL, copyrighted by AM&B on June 29, 1904, is a classic example of the chase motion picture. Apparently, AM&B produced it because of the enthusiastic audience reaction to their January motion picture called THE ESCAPED LUNATIC. Each follows the identical format. By this time, some film-makers understood that they were free from the limitations of a one-camera position stage play type of motion picture. Directors began to realize that by placing an obstacle between the camera and the oncoming actors, they could not only lengthen the scene but also add to the entertainment value of their films.

SOLE OWNERS,
THE BIOGRAPH. – THE MUTOSCOPE.

TELEPHONE: 1860 GRAMERCY.
CABLE ADDRESS: "MUTO"
LIEBER CODE.
WESTERN UNION CODE.

American Mutoscope and Biograph Company

FOREIGN CONNECTIONS.
LONDON - PARIS.
AMSTERDAM.
BERLIN - VIENNA.
JOHANNESBURG.
BRUSSELS - BOMBAY.
MILAN.
SYDNEY.

11 E. Fourteenth St.

New York, August 31, 1904.

To Our Customers:

In view of the fact that our great comedy-hit "PERSONAL" has been imitated by a firm of American film makers, we have decided to mark it Class B and offer it to the trade at 12 cts per foot--Length 371 ft.

This film has just finished a four weeks run at Keith's Union Square Theatre--two weeks longer than any film produced during the past two years. So successful has it been that our high-minded competitors, the same concern that has filled columns of "Clipper" space with warnings against the Philadelphia copyist, have deliberately appropriated our original idea, changing the advertisement upon which the story is founded in but one or two words, for the purpose of avoiding our copyrights, and reproducing the action of our film as nearly as they could.

We appeal to all fair-minded business men not to give their support to such dishonorable methods.

AMERICAN MUTOSCOPE AND BIOGRAPH CO.

PERSONAL became so popular that within a few short weeks a film with the unbelievably long title of HOW A FRENCH NOBLEMAN GOT A WIFE THROUGH THE NEW YORK HERALD PERSONAL COLUMNS was released by the Thomas A. Edison Company, an action that was not appreciated by AM&B. One hundred feet longer, the Edison version followed exactly the same story line as PERSONAL and even was made on the same location. By October, the Edison company also had made an almost exact copy of AM&B's popular January, 1904, release, THE ESCAPED LUNATIC, which they titled MANIAC CHASE and filmed at the identical locale. PERSONAL was directed by Wallace McCutcheon and photographed by G. W. "Billy" Bitzer who had been an AM&B staff cameraman since 1898.

The American Mutoscope & Biograph Company was displeased when the Edison company remade PERSONAL. Their annoyance was increased, however, when they discovered that nearly 100 miles to the south in Philadelphia, Siegmund Lubin was distributing the same film under the title NEW VERSION OF PERSONAL. The Edison company took the trouble to remake the film, but their southern neighbor simply ran it through one of his optical printers, thus saving the cost of production. Lubin knew, because he was an artist at it himself, that film duping, besides being less costly, was almost a survival necessity in the film distribution field.

Siegmund Lubin started out in the motion picture business in the city of Philadelphia where, by 1904, he owned four theatres on its main thoroughfare. He also owned one of the most complete film labs extant and, as a means of selling more prints of his films, he took a one-page ad in a trade paper of 1904 indicating that for $99 anyone could start in the motion picture exhibition business. For that amount of money, Lubin would sell him a projector of his own manufacture and, if he hurried, the embryonic exhibitor would get a Victor phonograph free which would provide music for Lubin's films. Records, of course, were $2 each. As an additional point of security, Lubin's projector would accept no film but those he produced.

During the years that moving pictures grew from a peep show affair into a billion dollar industry, "Pop" Lubin was very much in evidence. Back in 1897, when he could not get the Corbett-Fitzsimmons fight films for his theaters, he was resourceful enough to hire a couple of stevedores and photograph a reproduction. The action was guided by a director who read aloud the newspaper account of the fight, round by round. This film was so financially successful that Lubin continued the practice of making reproductions, as many as 34 in a single year, for some time.

In the same year (1897), R. G. Hollaman filmed a version of the Passion play on a New York roof top. Not to be outdone, Lubin made his version in the backyard of a house in Philadelphia. In fact, the list of films copyrighted by Lubin reads rather like a combined AM&B, Edison, and Melies catalog, including a motion picture that was quite popular in 1904 called THE GREAT TRAIN ROBBERY.

THE BOLD BANK ROBBERY

If it seemed like a good idea, and other film producers were making money, "Pop" Lubin simply appropriated the title and remade or duped the motion picture. Despite his deserved reputation as the foremost plagiarist in the film business, Lubin was there first in some instances. Copyright records show that he made a film called A TRIP TO THE MOON three years before Melies produced his well-known picture of the same title; Lubin copyrighted TOM, TOM, THE PIPER'S SON two years before AM&B, and his UNCLE TOM'S CABIN was released three months before the one Edwin S. Porter made for the Edison company.

Siegmund Lubin was not solely a film producer. He also manufactured cameras, printers, projectors, and film developing equipment. As late as 1912, Lubin was considered to be the number one technician in the motion picture field, a distinction that may have stemmed from his European training in the optical business.

While Lubin did not take the trouble to remake AM&B's film, PERSONAL, he was a very capable film-maker whenever he chose. One instance of his capability is his motion picture, THE BOLD BANK ROBBERY, copyrighted on July 25, 1904. The 277-foot motion picture is another chase film, but this time in dramatic form. THE BOLD BANK ROBBERY begins with a half three-shot of the principals who conspire to rob a bank. After they have done so, the villains make their getaway in a Packard touring car of the era. Forced to abandon this, they take to Philadelphia street cars, tunnels, and railroads for the chase scenes. The capture of the bandits is eventually accomplished when the police telegraph ahead to the next railroad station.

In the last scene, the camera cuts to another three-shot, this time with the culprits in the unattractive stripes of prison uniform instead of their former top hats and evening clothes.

THE BOLD BANK ROBBERY was photographed by Jack Frawley, a versatile cameraman, who also served as Lubin's general manager and director. Frawley, an imaginative individual, usually thought up the stories for Lubin's motion pictures.

The Bewitched Traveller

A NOVELTY IN TRICK PICTURES

Hepworth & Co.'s Latest London Triumph

(INTERNATIONAL COPYRIGHT)

Length 272 Feet   **Price $49.00**

The old style trick pictures which were popular so long, and which have only lost their popularity because of a lack of novelties, have been surpassed in a most surprising way by the celebrated London firm, Hepworth & Co., in their newest production, ''THE BEWITCHED TRAVELLER.''

This it a straight comedy picture, without the magicians, ballet girls and the rest of the familiar characters. A young gentleman is traveling for pleasure.

In the first scene he is in the dining-room of an inn endeavoring to get a meal. The table fades away before his eyes and simultaneously appears on the opposite side of the room. He changes his seat and takes up a cup of coffee, but the table again fades away. Then, in anger, he goes into the street and stops a 'bus. He has no sooner taken his seat than the horses fade away. He dismounts and, with the other passengers, goes to the front to investigate. The entire 'bus and the passengers also fade away. He tries to get on another 'bus, but it slides out from under him, and he rolls headlong into the street. He then goes to the railroad station and tries to board a train. The train comes in, and before he can board it, it fades away. Another train goes through at *full speed* and vanishes in a similar manner. The young man then determines to try a 'bus again and sits down on his valise at the roadside. A 'bus comes, but just before it reaches him it fades and goes by like a vision, and he never sees it. The young man, now thoroughly distracted, goes crazy and dances about the road waving his arms over his head as if pursued by a swarm of imps. As he does this he vanishes, and his valise follows him in a puff of smoke.

This film must be seen to be appreciated. It is a continuous series of laughs and astounding tricks throughout.

Produced and Controlled Exclusively by the

American Mutoscope & Biograph Company,

11 EAST 14th STREET, NEW YORK CITY.

THE BEWITCHED TRAVELLER

THE BEWITCHED TRAVELLER is being discussed here because it was copyrighted in the United States by AM&B on August 12, 1904, although this Hepworth comedy had been made in England some months earlier, where it proved quite popular with movie audiences. The 106-foot film is a good example of how far British film-makers had progressed in the realm of special effects, which were used to cause clothing, furniture, and public conveyances to disappear before the eyes of the harassed traveller.

By 1904 motion pictures were no longer such a novelty, and more and more persons went to see them as an everyday matter. Motion picture-makers had begun to learn their craft, and their films reflected improved pre-production thinking. Stories were selected on the basis of audience appeal, for experience had taught producers the type of film that sold tickets. About this time, motion picture-makers also began to advertise their films by distributing handbills in the neighborhood and occasionally through the newspapers.

THE MOONSHINER

In 1904, Edison and AM&B made three films within 30 days of one another for which there was no precedent, and yet each has an entirely different approach to movie-making. THE MOONSHINER, copyrighted by AM&B on August 19, 1904, is a dramatized documentation of the illegal practice of distilling whiskey without a Federal permit. A title describing what is to come precedes each of its ten scenes. This 394-foot film is by far the most ambitious surviving motion picture produced by AM&B up to that time. It was directed by Wallace McCutcheon, head director of AM&B, and photographed by Billy Bitzer. McCutcheon moved the camera many times while making the picture. On two occasions, he directed Bitzer to move the camera in for closeups — once in the death scene and once for an insert. In another instance, the camera was panned in order to hold the action together. The motion picture was photographed in Scarsdale, New York. One of the actors was Wallace McCutcheon, son of the director; another was Harold Vosburg.

The Moonshiner

EUROPEAN REST CURE

Copyrighted on September 1, 1904 and photographed by Edwin S. Porter for the Thomas A. Edison Company, EUROPEAN REST CURE is a humorous film that follows an especially written story about an old gaffer (played by Joseph Hart), who is sent by his family on a sea voyage and European tour for his health. Every scene in the 402-foot film is directed to give the hero of the story a bad time and to see that rest is one thing he does not get. Sets were built to resemble a cabin of a ship at sea, Italian ruins, Egyptian pyramids, etc., and all added to our hero's dilemma. Instead of the customary painted backdrops of the day, all of the sets have dimension and are practical by today's standards.

Newsreel film photographed in 1897 and 1898 was edited into the ship departure and arrival scenes photographed for the motion picture itself. In one scene, the camera is rocked to give the illusion of rough going at sea for the passenger, possibly an innovation. Edwin S. Porter also employed stop action special effects whenever it seemed to add humor to the story.

THE WIDOW AND THE ONLY MAN

The opportunity for making good films was unlimited in 1904, for there was little precedent and no rules to limit the film-maker. The only objective was to complete a picture as fast as possible that would sell.

Whether AM&B's THE WIDOW AND THE ONLY MAN, copyrighted on September 8, 1904, was a success at the box office is not known, but this 318-foot comedy certainly contributed several new camera uses in telling a story. The film begins with a title that introduces the widow in a portrait one-shot. Then the "only man" is also introduced in the same manner. The locale of the motion picture is a summer resort overpopulated by vacationing women of various ages and sizes. The hero of the picture apparently is the only eligible young man there. The story develops as the title implies, and the climax comes as the only man saves the widow when their canoe capsizes.

To show the delight on the rescued widow's face as she inspects some flowers sent to her by the hero, the director, Wallace McCutcheon, had Billy Bitzer move the camera from the establishing shot in to a tight closeup and back out again.

ROUNDING UP OF THE "YEGGMEN"

ROUNDING UP OF THE "YEGGMEN" was copyrighted by the Edison company on September 16, 1904, just eight days after AM&B copyrighted THE WIDOW AND THE ONLY MAN. These two films in no way resemble one another, but each contains an innovation in film-making, and each is an excellent example of the kind of motion picture a creative film-maker could produce even in the very early years.

The story of ROUNDING UP OF THE "YEGGMEN" is based on a bank robbery and a chase. Instead of the usual capture, Edwin S. Porter ended his film in the manner of "The Lady and the Tiger," by letting the audience decide for themselves whether the bandits who were fleeing in a stolen locomotive actually were killed when it hit another train head-on. For this scene, Porter made use of some previously photographed film of a collision between two locomotives.

In this motion picture, Porter's growth and individuality as a film-maker becomes very evident. He demonstrates that he could establish a plot in the first few scenes of a picture and keep the story line going without depending upon fantasy, opticals, stop camera work, or titles. As a result, this 380-foot film is probably one of the best of his early efforts.

ROUNDING UP OF THE "YEGGMEN" is a complete and imaginative story. The first scenes show actor movement to a central point in front of a camera, with each actor contributing to the scene. From start to finish, Porter directed his actors and moved the camera so that his audience always was aware of what was about to happen, as well as of what was going on at the time. His meticulous design of sets made the transfer from exteriors to interiors readily believable by the audience. When it is taken into consideration how little control motion picture-makers of this period had over the chemical capacities of their film, the result of this one-man production is nothing short of extraordinary.

THE HERO OF LIAO YANG

World affairs, then as now, often provide film-makers with an idea for a motion picture. Russia and Japan were at war in 1904, and Liaoyang, Manchuria, was the scene of a Japanese victory over the Russians. Out of this circumstance, AM&B made an extraordinary motion picture that was 531 feet long. It was titled THE HERO OF LIAO YANG. The copyright date was September 22, 1904.

The story is of an actual act of heroism performed by the eldest son of a Japanese family. He was an officer/messenger, who feigned death to elude his captors and allowed himself to be buried alive. After his rescue by a fellow soldier, who had observed the burial, the officer completed his mission.

Camera panning was used in THE HERO OF LIAO YANG to hold the action together in long scenes. This type of camera usage was extremely rare in films made in the first few years of motion picture production. The special effects and pyrotechnics of the battle scenes would do credit to a "powder monkey" at a major film studio today.

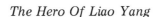
The Hero Of Liao Yang

Another thing that must not be overlooked — again referring to the date — is that THE HERO OF LIAO YANG is at least a two-reel film. If the original production schedule called for two reels, then it is the earliest of the two-reelers restored from paper prints. If it was not planned, but happened only because the cameraman used up two reels of film, then it should be given acclaim as an exceptional motion picture but not as a two-reeler. However, from the way the first reel ends and the second begins, as well as the way it was advertised by AM&B in their handbills, this motion picture originally was intended to be more than one reel in length.

Some scenes of THE HERO OF LIAO YANG were filmed in Colonel William Verbeck's Japanese garden on the grounds of St. John's Military Academy in Manlius, New York. Biograph records do not identify the cameraman of this unusual piece of film making, but we have been fortunate enough to learn from the Colonel's cousin, Bob Verbeck, who witnessed the event, it was none other than Billy Bitzer.

AM&B production records do show, however, that Bitzer had been on the grounds of St. John's Military Academy a few months earlier, photographing a documentary of the Academy. While he was there, Bitzer made use of the students and equipment to make a film of another Japanese victory over the Russians called THE BATTLE OF THE YALU, featuring Colonel Verbeck in the role of a Cossack. The film was copyrighted by AM&B in four parts in March of 1904.

REVENGE!
A RAILWAY TRAGEDY

Our practice of introducing films in order of their American copyright date now brings us to motion pictures made in England by L. Gaumont & Co. and distributed in the United States by AM&B. They are REVENGE!, copyrighted on October 1, 1904, and A RAILWAY TRAGEDY, copyrighted nine days later. AM&B imported no films that had not already been successfully exhibited abroad. Therefore these two motion pictures actually were made some months earlier than the date of American copyright.

These British films, too, are of a realistic nature and show very clearly that a considerable amount of preparation and pre-production planning went into their making.

The words, "This is a thriller," were used by AM&B to describe the 149-foot REVENGE! in an October 17, 1904, bulletin announcing the availability of some new English films. REVENGE! is a savage melodrama of a young man who comes upon a police officer attempting to seduce his wife against her will. After the fight that follows, the husband is taken off to jail. He escapes by sliding down a rope, and at least eight different camera positions are used to photograph the exciting chase scenes that follow. The film ends as the hero strangles the villain, but not before the audience follows the hero from the prison courtyard on a series of chases, climaxed by a battle during which the hero throws a number of policemen over a cliff, one by one, in his frenzied scramble to avoid capture.

Revenge!

The second Gaumont film, A RAILWAY TRAGEDY, is about a robbery and assault on an attractive young woman in a train compartment. During the attack the young woman is thrown from the train. The film ends with the capture of the villain on a station platform as he attempts to make his getaway. Several camera positions were used in photographing the 135-foot A RAILWAY TRAGEDY. When the train door opens during the attack scene, it is obvious that the railway compartment was a constructed set, as the landscape remains stationary.

Labels from eight original reels of PARSIFAL, an early Edison/Porter extravaganza. Term "scene" was used instead of "reel" or "part".

PARSIFAL

In 1865 a 21-year-old English peer by the name of Queensberry drafted the rules now used in boxing. One of his rules set a time limit on each round, previously governed only by the length of time it took one fighter to knock down the other. The motion picture industry had no Queensberry to set standards for them. It was sort of like Topsy, it just grew. Today's motion picture-makers have arrived at a standard length for one reel, with a standard number of feet of film in the reel. Much has been said about the director or film-making company that produced the "first" two- or multi-reel film. They were using today's standard of reel length.

However, by comparing the labels and the footage sent to the Library of Congress for copyright by Thomas A. Edison's film-maker, Edwin S. Porter, it is apparent that Porter believed motion pictures should be made in scenes, and that when an idea for a scene had been completed, the reel ended, whether it was 20 feet or 382 feet, as in the case of PARSIFAL.

Another of the values of the paper print restoration program is that now we are able to see such almost unknown motion pictures as PARSIFAL, copyrighted by Edison on October 13, 1904. Although it was probably the most ambitious and costly film made at the Edison company while Porter was in charge of production there, very few people ever saw it. Its release was short-lived, as this film was part of the first lawsuit that established the right of an author to prevent a motion picture being made from his script without his permission.

When Wagner's opera PARSIFAL opened at the Metropolitan Opera House in New York, it was immensely popular, and apparently it seemed like a good source for a motion picture. The film, when completed, was over 600 feet long, with eight episodes that varied in length from 20 feet to 382 feet, and it incorporated most of the production lessons that Porter had learned from making previous films. It is plain from the picture that the Edison company had planned to release phonograph records of the musical score with the film. Lacking music, the film has little entertainment value. All the actors do is to stand before the camera, or walk around in the stage area and gesture as if they were singing. While the public apparently was ready for sound pictures, the mechanical problems of synchronization of electric motors and amplification of sound had not been solved and so none were made.

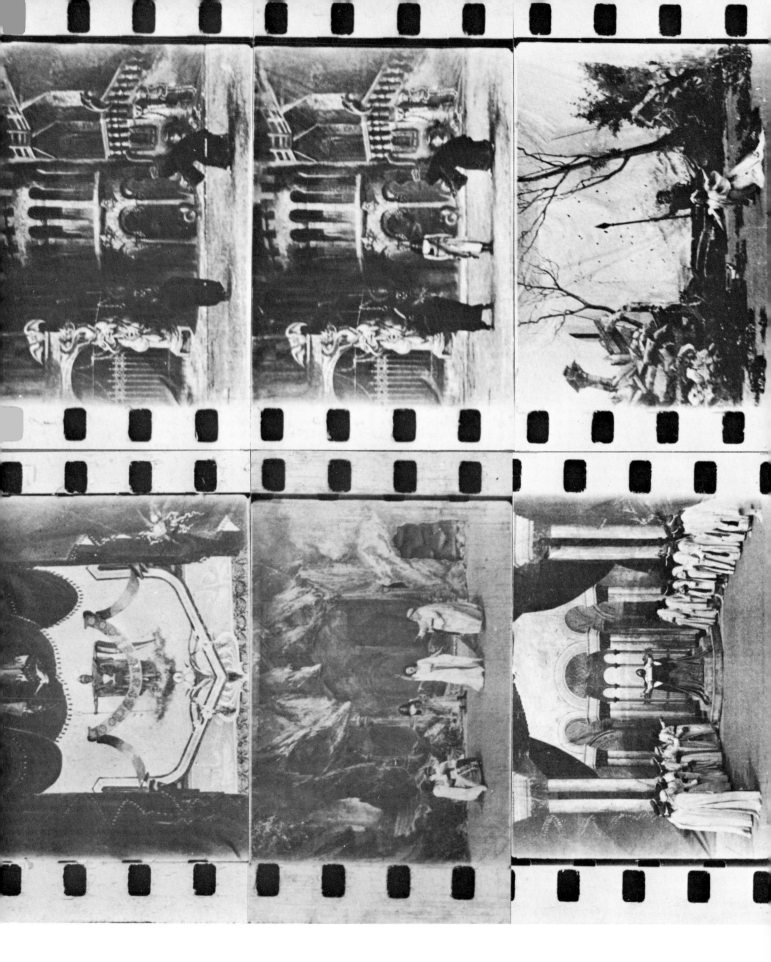

FORM NO. 1146   BULLETIN 36, Oct. 26, 1904

THE LOST CHILD

ANOTHER GREAT COMEDY CHASE

BY THE ORIGINATORS OF

" Personal " and " The Escaped Lunatic "

IN FULL CRY

BRIGHTER, FUNNIER AND BETTER

THAN THE OTHERS

FOUNDED ON FACT

Produced and Controlled Exclusively by the

American Mutoscope & Biograph Co.

11 East 14th Street, New York City.

THE LOST CHILD

The American Mutoscope & Biograph Company had made money by exhibiting foreign films and also by producing their own, the most successful of which were such comedy chase films as THE ESCAPED LUNATIC and PERSONAL, all with essentially the same format but with different locales.

AM&B's advertisement acclaimed their October 15, 1904, chase film, THE LOST CHILD, as "brighter, funnier and better than the others," and also stated that it was "founded on fact." One of the elements of the picture that AM&B did not mention in their handbill was the significance of the director's new use of a camera. Generally speaking, early chase films simply ended when the director felt he had crammed enough characters and funny situations into the amount of film allotted for the picture, but in the 231-foot film, THE LOST CHILD, a director saw an opportunity in a newspaper story to add a new twist to the usual stereotyped comedy format for a motion picture. To create a climax for THE LOST CHILD that was not employed in either THE ESCAPED LUNATIC or PERSONAL, he used a closeup to show that what was in the basket was not the lost child but a pet guinea pig. The part of the frantic mother was played by Kathryn Osterman. It was photographed in Brooklyn by G. W. Billy Bitzer, and in all probability directed by Wallace McCutcheon.

AN ENGLISHMAN'S TRIP TO PARIS FROM LONDON

Among the films that were made in England and distributed in the United States by AM&B that provide an insight into the English film-makers' ability to poke fun at themselves is a picture named AN ENGLISHMAN'S TRIP TO PARIS FROM LONDON, copyrighted by AM&B in the United States on October 28, 1904. The story is a simple one, photographed entirely outdoors, with the exception of one scene of a very large and obese woman who is stuck in a passageway and holds up a line of ticket buyers. The outdoor scenes are of the railway station, a paddle wheel Channel steamer, and a number of public buildings in and around Paris. The traveller is shown seeing the sights, absorbing culture, and taking pictures. The final scene in this 144-foot comedy shows the tourist seated at a sidewalk cafe where he drinks a glass of English stout, much to the amusement of the waiter who served him. This film is Hepworth's A TRIP TO PARIS, directed by Lewin Fitzhamon.

DECOYED

A complete contrast to the comedy, AN ENGLISHMAN'S TRIP TO PARIS FROM LONDON, DECOYED is an 108-foot social documentary that was copyrighted in the United States by AM&B on the same day as the previous film. DECOYED is about a young girl, a stranger in the city, who is abducted by a man, forced to live in squalor, and solicit on the city streets. The finale of the film is rather humorous from today's point of view, for it shows the young man who rescues the girl from her sordid surroundings removing his coat and very carefully laying it aside before administering a beating to the patiently waiting villain.

Handbills issued by AM&B offered "new English subjects," but did not always identify the maker of the film, nor give the date it was photographed. In the years that have elapsed since the first edition of this book, we have been able to confirm our feeling that DECOYED was a Hepworth production. This little film was released in Great Britain as LOST, STOLEN OR STRAYED. The director was Lewin Fitzhamon, who also played the villain in the picture. Dolly Lupone took the part of the girl.

FORM NO. 1148   BULLETIN No. 37, Nov. 28, 1904

THE SUBURBANITE

A Comedy Production in Seven Scenes

Wherein are Shown the Trials and Tribulations of a City Man Who is Enticed From His Cozy Flat by the Real Estate Agent ⌀ ⌀ ⌀ ⌀ ⌀

MOVING IN

"Why Pay Rent in the City?"
"Own a Sweet Little Home in the Country"

LENGTH 718 FEET

Produced and Controlled Exclusively by the

American Mutoscope & Biograph Co.

11 East 14th Street, New York City.

THE SUBURBANITE

Today it is not unusual to see in the credits of a motion picture, "written especially for the screen," but it is difficult to establish exactly when this practice began. On November 11, 1904, AM&B made a motion picture called THE SUBURBANITE from a previously written story that they considered suitable for both the stage and a motion picture and was so copyrighted.

THE SUBURBANITE, a 291-foot long situation comedy, is the story of a city dweller who, fed up with urban living, succumbs to the "own a sweet little home in the country" pitch of a real estate salesman. Each of the scenes begins with a title that sets the mood and tells what is to happen. At the end of the picture, the family is shown leaving their home in the country, not even taking the trouble to pack, and heading gratefully back to the city.

It is interesting that in a previously mentioned film, THE STORY THE BIOGRAPH TOLD, a British-made motion picture camera, the Moy-Basty, was used as a prop. In one of the episodes in THE SUBURBANITE, the distinctive cases for that very same motion picture camera were left on the lawn, which would lead to the conclusion that not all AM&B motion pictures were photographed with a Biograph camera. Both pictures were filmed by A. E. Weed, a staff cameraman for AM&B for several years. The part of "The Suburbanite" was played by John Troiano.

THE EX-CONVICT

We often read that Edwin S. Porter's work was influenced by French film-makers, but there is only one of his films among all of those restored from the paper prints that would support this theory. It is JACK AND THE BEANSTALK, already discussed. By the time Porter produced THE EX-CONVICT for Edison, he had been making motion pictures for about five years. His films show that it was beginning to occur to him that a camera could be used not only to make motion pictures for entertainment but also to acquaint the public with a social problem or an injustice, such as the British had been doing for about four years. Both THE EX-CONVICT and THE KLEPTOMANIAC, which will be discussed later, are protests against the social structure of the day.

THE EX-CONVICT is the story of a man forced back into a life of crime when his prison record prevents his obtaining employment. When the ex-convict is caught as he burglarizes the house owned by the man whose daughter he had saved from an oncoming automobile, the daughter recognizes him. Because of his act of bravery, the ex-convict's fortunes now take a turn for the better.

THE EX-CONVICT, copyrighted by Edison on November 19, 1904, is a filmed story of approximately 800 35mm feet, divided into eight episodes, each with an explanatory title preceding the action of the scene. Each episode or scene varies in length, for apparently it was Porter's custom to use only enough film for each segment to effectively convey to the audience the action described in the foregoing title. Some episodes were 50 feet long, while others were as long as 200 feet. The snow scene is the only instance in THE EX-CONVICT where Porter employs special effects, although his earlier work shows he was a master of all of the camera tricks then known to the film-maker. The story is predominant in THE EX-CONVICT, the camera being used only as a tool to tell that story.

A RACE FOR A KISS

The paper print restoration program has made it possible to see three primitive films made by the Hepworth Manufacturing Company of Walton-on-Thames in England. All were imported for exhibition in the United States, and all were copyrighted by AM&B on November 28, 1904, but there is reason to believe that they were made several years earlier.

Little information is available on these three short comedies, other than that which can be gleaned from looking at and comparing them. A RACE FOR A KISS is 80 feet long and involves a race between an automobile and its driver, and a horse and its jockey, for the privilege of a kiss from a lovely young lady. On the first approach, the horse and the automobile are neck and neck. In the second run-through, the automobile is leading. In the third and last lap, the horse and rider are in front. The actors were directed to approach the camera from a distance to prolong each scene and build up suspense. As an extra touch of humor, the driver is seen being lead off by a policeman, leaving his car abandoned by the roadside. A RACE FOR A KISS was directed by Lewin Fitzhamon, who also took the part of the jockey, and the female lead was played by Dolly Lupone.

THE OTHER SIDE OF THE HEDGE

The 40-foot comedy, THE OTHER SIDE OF THE HEDGE, another of the three English films in this group, very definitely indicates pre-production planning. The establishing scene shows three actors, a young boy, a young girl, and their considerably overweight chaperone at a picnic. In the second and last scene, the camera was moved from the establishing shot to show how the chaperone had been fooled into believing her charges were behaving properly. THE OTHER SIDE OF THE HEDGE was released on December 16, 1904, by AM&B under the title OVER THE HEDGE. Again the director was Lewin Fitzhamon.

The plot of THE LOVER'S RUSE is contained in only 22 feet of film and is acted by a young couple photographed from a single camera position. A suitor pretends to take poison when the young woman with whom he is strolling spurns his love. She attempts to revive him and is kissed for her efforts. The picture was released in England under the title POISON OR WHISKEY, and it also was directed by Lewin Fitzhamon.

THE KLEPTOMANIAC

The script for THE KLEPTOMANIAC was written to acquaint the audience with flaws in the established social system, and it attempts to convey the idea that there is one sort of civil justice for the rich and another for the poor. THE KLEPTOMANIAC was copyrighted by the Edison company on February 4, 1905, only three months after THE EX-CONVICT and differs from that film in that the audience sees parallel stories as the film progresses, while THE EX-CONVICT has only one principal character.

The opening scene in THE KLEPTOMANIAC shows an obviously wealthy woman entering a New York department store where she is apprehended for shoplifting. Allowed to drive off to jail in her own carriage, she is arraigned before a magistrate who offers her his chair. Her preferential treatment continues, and she is released. The other characters in the story are two starving children and their destitute mother, who is arrested when she steals a loaf of bread from a basket on the sidewalk in front of a grocery store. Edwin S. Porter, who directed this film, used a camera to show how the poor woman was humiliated by the police, who take her off in their van to the same magistrate. The mother receives a jail sentence, the magistrate having failed to take into consideration that she will leave two young children unattended. As an epilogue to the picture, the goddess of justice is portrayed, one eye covered by a bandage, as she holds a scale that tilts in favor of a bag of money.

Both THE EX-CONVICT and THE KLEPTOMANIAC were films with a message, but they differ a great deal in production procedure. The paper prints disclose that THE EX-CONVICT was made in separate episodes with a title preceding each, while THE KLEPTOMANIAC was on one 315-foot reel of film, with a single overall title.

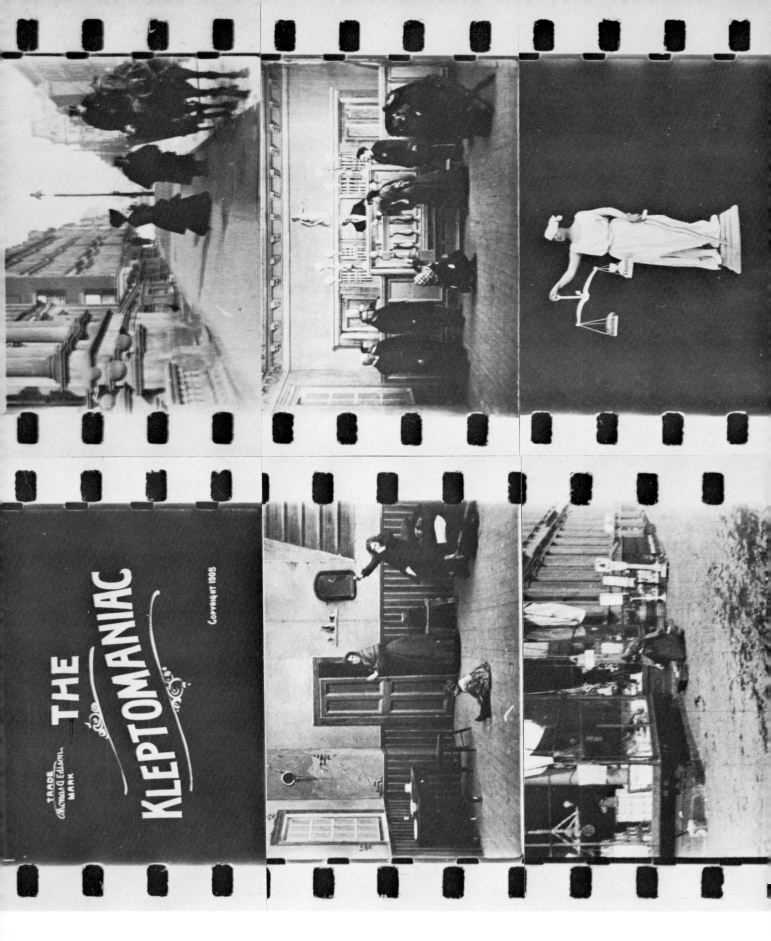

THE SEVEN AGES

THE SEVEN AGES, also made by Edwin S. Porter for the Edison company in February of 1905, represents still another Porter approach to film-making. Begun as a photographic research project, when completed it proved to be sufficiently novel to be released for public showing.

The main title on this 224-foot film is THE SEVEN AGES. It is broken up into eight parts, each of a different length. Each label on the eight rolls of paper sent to the Library of Congress on February 27, 1905 for copyright bears the same Edison production number, even though each scene was numbered individually from one to eight and was assigned a separate copyright number.

The eight reels or scenes of THE SEVEN AGES are titled "Infancy, Playmates, Schoolmates, Lovers, The Soldier, The Judge, Second Childhood," and the last scene, showing a woman of indeterminate age holding a cat, has a large question mark under its title, "What Age?" This was the only one of the eight episodes that did not have camera movement from the establishing shot in to a portrait or waist closeup.

The action of "The Soldier" and "Lovers" is identical, except for an exposure change. In "The Judge" and "Second Childhood," Porter wanted to find out how to do a one-source-of-light sequence to create the impression of nighttime with sufficient brilliance for proper exposure, so he experimented with a mirror that reflected the sun from a tray of water in the fireplace scenes. The result was a very definite photographic innovation.

TOM, TOM, THE PIPER'S SON

Research into the records of the American Mutoscope & Biograph Company for the first few years that they were making motion pictures for projection makes it clear that the films that made the most money were the "chase" pictures.

TOM, TOM, THE PIPER'S SON was considered by the producers at AM&B to be the "original" chase story. Their handbill lauds the picture for its length, says it was based on the most familiar and laughable incident in the whole list of childhood tales and, further, that the sets and costumes were copied from Hogarth prints of the period. As another sales point, AM&B also mentioned that the film was photographed in their all electric studio. There are no exterior scenes in it, and this would support their claim. The limitations the stage imposed on the camera showed in the finished product, as the film was little more than a series of eight scenes photographed in front of constructed sets. The large cast ran from stage left to stage right, and after the last person left the camera's view, there was a direct cut to the next set with no titles between scenes.

G. W. Bitzer, the cameraman, used only one camera trick in the film, and that was to run the camera backwards in order to get the runaway boy and stolen pig up a chimney. Despite all the time, money, and pre-production planning lavished on TOM, TOM, THE PIPER'S SON, it lacked the charm of an outdoor chase film. It was 268 feet long and was copyrighted by AM&B on March 9, 1905.

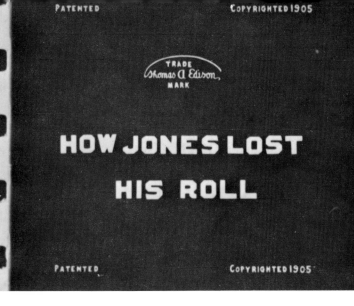

HOW JONES LOST HIS ROLL

The stir that the amusing animated titles of the Edison film HOW JONES LOST HIS ROLL caused when it was released was nothing less than sensational. The format of this 300-foot motion picture is similar to Porter's earlier film, THE SEVEN AGES, as it also is made up of separate scenes, each with a title that informs the viewer of the action to come, but for the titles of HOW JONES LOST HIS ROLL, the inventive Porter used the stop motion device he had developed to surmount an early exposure problem.

As each scene of this humorous film begins, the viewer sees scrambled letters that smoothly, and with seeming purpose, quickly form into a sentence to become the title of a scene. To add a little something extra to one title, Porter deliberately misspelled a word and then had the delinquent letter scurry across the frame to its proper place; in another, he used cutouts of a pair of hands about to clasp.

History has it that Porter's competitors snooped for almost a year before discovering his secret, and for a period of time after that there was a deluge of motion pictures titled with moving letters. There is no earlier example in the paper print collection of titles made with stop action than Porter's HOW JONES LOST HIS ROLL. HOW JONES was copyrighted on March 27, 1905, and is made up of seven scenes of varying lengths, each with a separate copyright number. Porter again followed his practice of ending a scene when the action justified it; there was no set length to any of them.

THE NIHILISTS

"With the Japanese in the East hammering to pieces the armies of the Czar, and with revolution fomenting throughout the empire, Russia demands the attention of the whole world," was the lead sentence in the handbill advertising AM&B's "latest magnificent film production," THE NIHILISTS, copyrighted by them on March 28, 1905. This 390-foot motion picture consisted of seven scenes, each preceded by a title, and told of an aristocratic family torn asunder by political intrigue. The film goes on to show the conspiracy of the remaining members of the family intent upon avenging their father, who had been taken from them, tortured, and then exiled to Siberia.

The seventh scene of THE NIHILISTS, entitled "Vengeance," was one of the best planned production scenes made by AM&B in that era. A full width set was constructed to represent the grand ballroom of the governor's palace. Then, to show how the ballroom looked after the explosion of the bomb thrown by the heroine, another set, depicting the wreckage, was constructed. In order to mask the transfer from the whole set to the damaged one, a smoke bomb was set off between the camera and the sets. The film ends by showing the heroine kneeling, arms stretched heavenward.

The cameraman of THE NIHILISTS was F. S. Armitage, who photographed the exteriors in Grantwood, New Jersey, and the interiors in the Biograph studio in New York City.

THE WHOLE DAM FAMILY AND THE DAM DOG

When Edwin S. Porter made THE WHOLE DAM FAMILY AND THE DAM DOG for Edison, he varied a format previously used by AM&B to begin their motion picture THE WIDOW AND THE ONLY MAN of identifying and naming the principals in the cast by photographing them in a head-and-shoulder closeup. Porter's variation was that he brought out the personality of each of his characters by directing them to do a piece of stage business while they were being introduced to the movie audience in the same sort of closeup. Porter introduced the canine member of the Dam family in another way, however, by using the animation technique he had perfected for the titles in HOW JONES LOST HIS ROLL two months before. This time, Porter animated a paper cutout of a dog with a tail that wagged and dispersed the letters of the title. It is quite obvious in the closeups that makeup was employed to give the members of the cast a family resemblance.

Porter followed the individual closeups with a group shot of the whole cast. The final scene in the picture shows the family at a sit-down dinner that is interrupted by the antics of the Dam dog, who evidently caused the retake of a scene when he was so carried away by the importance of his part that he did not perform as directed. THE WHOLE DAM FAMILY AND THE DAM DOG, copyrighted on May 31, 1905, is 138 feet long, including the retake. Most of the film was expended on introducing the cast.

THE WHOLE DAM FAMILY AND THE DAM DOG is the last of Porter's pictures made between 1901 and 1905 to be discussed in this book. Every one made a contribution to the technique of motion picture-making and to the history of the art. Each was an individual and different way to communicate through the use of a motion picture camera.

RESCUED BY ROVER

Right from the start, there were many film producing companies in England, but not all continued to make motion pictures. Some found manufacturing film-making equipment more lucrative. For the first few years of projection, British motion picture cameras and printers enjoyed considerable popularity throughout the world, for they were fine examples of mechanical craftsmanship. The British also spearheaded early research in motion picture color.

For the first ten years of motion picture projection, films produced abroad were about the same length as they were in America, for film-makers all over the world had discovered they could tell a story in four to six minutes that would interest an audience. Moving the camera from place to place was not unusual in British films, and the practice of directing actors toward or away from the camera position in order to lengthen a scene was common. Stop camera action, in-the-camera dissolves, and the closeup were used whenever a director felt it was necessary, and dummies were frequently substituted for live actors in stunt scenes. It is quite evident that most of the sets were constructed out of doors instead of being artificially lighted. Lack of readily available electric power, as well as the expense involved, probably had a great deal to do with this.

British film-makers used unexposed film manufactured in their own factories or what they bought in France and sometimes even from American sources, and they were subject to the same manner of mechanical problems that troubled American film-makers of the time. If a producer made a film that was exceptionally popular, he was forced to make the motion picture over again in order to have a new negative. The original negative could be run through a printer only a few times before the sprocket holes became elongated, and the emulsion badly scratched.

A print from such a negative did not project well and was unsteady on the screen. This is what happened in the instance of Hepworth's RESCUED BY ROVER. It was so successful that during its four or five years of exhibition, more than 400 prints, from different negatives, were made and sold.

An idea of how fantastically popular RESCUED BY ROVER was may be gathered from a survey made by William N. Selig, pioneer Chicago film-maker, for the American publication, THE FILM INDEX, one of the largest trade papers of the time. Selig says that Williamson, a British camera manufacturer and film-maker, told him that the highest number of prints made by them of any one subject was 29, which they had sold.

Laboratory practices had not advanced to the point where prints made from duplicate negatives were as satisfactory as those made from the original negatives. Consequently, in order to get more negatives, the whole production had to be rephotographed which may be the reason why accounts of RESCUED BY ROVER differ. Careful examination of the print deposited with the Library of Congress indicates that it was made from a copy made from a print of the first production of RESCUED BY ROVER. AM&B, who distributed this 195-foot drama in the United States, copyrighted it here on August 19, 1905.

RESCUED BY ROVER was made in England at the Walton-on-Thames studio of Cecil Hepworth. The plot concerns the kidnapping of an infant by a gypsy and the subsequent rescue of the child with the aid of the family dog. Rover is photographed as he runs through city streets, finds the baby, returns home, and leads his master to the gypsy's quarters. The last scene shows the happy family group together again. At the beginning and end of the film, the camera moves in for a closeup.

As mentioned elsewhere in this book, early film makers very often utilized members of their family in their motion pictures.

The scenario of RESCUED BY ROVER was written by Mrs. Cecil Hepworth; she also plays the part of the mother in the film. Cecil Hepworth himself was the father, while their infant daughter Barbara, perhaps unwittingly, was the kidnapped infant. The "star" of the production was the Hepworth dog Blair.

Actor/director Lewin Fitzhamon was the director. May Clark played the nursemaid. The parts of the soldier and the gypsy were taken by Mr. and Mrs. Sebastian Smith, reputedly the first British actors ever paid to appear in a film.

FINE FEATHERS MAKE FINE BIRDS

Another British film imported by AM&B was FINE FEATHERS MAKE FINE FRIENDS, copyrighted by them on August 25, 1905. The motion picture either gained or lost during its trip to the United States, for somehow the title was changed to FINE FEATHERS MAKE FINE BIRDS.

It is a fast-moving, amusing comedy. The plot has all the elements of a chase, but it was unusual for the time to employ an automobile and some motorbikes. The story begins with two couples out for a stroll near a country estate somewhere in England who become so enchanted with a large touring car that they decide to take it for a joy ride. The remainder of the film shows various incidents of their escapade, and the amusing problems that confront the pursuing policemen who apparently cannot ride their motorbikes very well.

The chase takes the pursued and the pursuers through the English countryside, along country roads, and there are stops in two villages for refreshment and street dancing. The chase comes to an abrupt end when the stolen car runs into a lake and the joy riders are captured by the police. FINE FEATHERS is 210 feet long.

FINE FEATHERS MAKE FINE BIRDS was released in Great Britain in July of 1905 under still another title: WILLIE AND TIM IN THE MOTOR CAR. The producer was Clarendon. The picture was directed by Percy Stow.

The American Mutoscope & Biograph Company was the only legally accepted competition the Edison motion picture organization had in America until after the patent suits were resolved in the first decade of the 20th century. Had Mr. Edison agreed to the expansion proposal made by his co-worker, William K. Laurie Dickson, prior to his leaving Edison's employ in April of 1895, the American Mutoscope & Biograph Company probably never would have been founded. As it was, Dickson, together with some financial and engineering brains, organized AM&B, Edison's chief rival until motion picture projectors became mechanically feasible.

The motion picture cameras of these two companies accomplished the same end, even if in a different mechanical manner, but the viewing devices for these two machines in no way resembled one another in their design or operation. In their primitive stages, before projectors were invented, both could be described as peephole viewing machines; that is where the resemblance stopped. In Edison's Kinetoscope, the viewer saw a print made from the original negative with a light behind it. A revolving shutter with a slot allowed him to see the picture on the print at intervals of approximately 20 per second. AM&B's Mutoscope used a series of still pictures made from the original negative and fastened, in the same order as photographed, to a hub similar to spokes on a wheel. Thus, when put into motion, the effect, because of the viewer's persistence of vision, was similar to that seen in Edison's Kinetoscope.

AM&B's practice of making motion pictures for the flip card viewing device lasted for many years, even after they also began making films for projection. Some of the flip card Mutoscopes occasionally can be seen to this day in penny arcades throughout the world, even though the company that invented them went out of existence before World War I. At one time, Mutoscopes were so popular that at least six motion picture cameramen, including a man who was to become famous, George W. "Billy" Bitzer, were kept busy supplying the demand.

The AM&B moving picture camera operated on the same general principle as the Edison machine, for it used flexible film, had a revolving shutter, and the unexposed film left one magazine and ended up exposed in another. However, there were several specific mechanical differences, the main one being that the Biograph camera perforated its own film, while the Edison machine used pre-perforated raw stock with eight perforations per frame.

Moving picture film used by Edison and most of the other moving picture manufacturers of the world was never more than 35mm wide, but the Biograph company at first didn't accept this width as standard for their film. Some of their film widths exceeded 70mm with sprocket holes on framelines and some on the edges to fit the specially designed viewer built to accept only Biograph productions. AM&B manufactured few projectors, and those were used mainly in the capitals of Europe and in large cities in the United States. Their projectors were not only heavy and cumbersome, but they also proved to be difficult to operate and expensive to use, as the film traveled through the projector in excess of 40 frames per second, or at more than twice the speed of other projectors. Another difference was that the film was transported through the Biograph machines by rubber rollers, while in the Edison machine this was effected by geared, sprocketed wheels, a method still in use today.

Apparently there were three reasons for AM&B clinging so tenaciously to their camera that perforated its own film. First, their patent for the film-perforating camera was not an infringement of Edison's camera, the Kinetograph. Second, it was a good protection against the trade practice of competitors duping their motion pictures, and, third, the sales policy of AM&B was to contract with a theater owner to furnish not only films but also a projector and a projectionist for a specific length of time.

AM&B showed no signs of joining the group of producers and exhibitors who used the 35mm film that was fast becoming the standard for the industry until they began representing European film manufacturers in America about May of 1903 with, as they advertised, "standard 35mm films with sprocket holes." The changeover to standard 35mm film widths for their own productions did not take place until approximately September, one year later.

FORM NO. 1192 BULLETIN No. 53, November 8, 1905

THE GREAT
JEWEL MYSTERY

A PINKERTON DETECTIVE STORY
IN BIOGRAPH PICTURES

Sherlock Holmes Outdone

THE JEWEL CASKET

SOLUTION OF THE SEASON'S SENSATION

LENGTH 651 FEET, CLASS "A"

Produced and Controlled Exclusively by the

American Mutoscope & Biograph Co.

11 East 14th Street, New York City.

THE GREAT JEWEL MYSTERY

Throughout the history of motion pictures actual cases from the files of law-enforcement agencies have been a popular source of stories about which to make films. This practice has continued on into television. THE GREAT JEWEL MYSTERY is a film made by AM&B as their solution to what was probably the greatest theft of its kind up until that time in the history of the New York Police Department. In 1905 a jewel case was stolen from a mail car during transit from New York City to Newport, R. I. According to AM&B's theory of how the particularly baffling robbery was accomplished, the thieves gained access to the mail car by the ruse of shipping a casket allegedly containing a dead body. Instead, it contained a very-much-alive robber who perpetrated the theft, and when the casket was removed from the mail car, the jewels went with him.

All of the scenes in THE GREAT JEWEL MYSTERY begin with a title that describes the action to follow, and there are several technical innovations in the film. There is a matte shot, or double exposure, that runs throughout the mail car episode, and there is a unique bit of set construction in the scene following the title "The Capture." A pole, or upright, is so placed that the camera will convey the idea to the audience that a wall exists. There is none. This undoubtedly was done to allow the electric lights to shine on the action. An actual wall would have blocked the illumination entirely.

Another technique of the cameraman's craft employed in THE GREAT JEWEL MYSTERY was, generally speaking, mechanically impossible at that time. It consisted of intercutting film from two different cameras in the same motion picture. One camera was operated by Billy Bitzer and the other by F. A. Dobson. The intercutting was made possible by a printer that could vary its frameline relationship to the film sprocket hole. In 1905 motion picture camera manufacturers gave little thought to standardization nor did motion picture producers demand it. Theatres combined the product of several motion picture cameras on a single reel. In order to get good projection of a reel of film, the projectionist had to adjust the frameline in the projector to take care of variances. This problem was eliminated by the new printer and, later, by standardization of film measurements and equipment.

The 268-foot film carries the title THE MYSTERY OF THE MISSING JEWEL CASKET although it was copyrighted by AM&B on October 23, 1905 as THE GREAT JEWEL MYSTERY. It was photographed in three days at Sound Beach, Connecticut, and in AM&B's New York City studio.

FORM NO. 1195   BULLETIN No. 56, November 13, 1905

A KENTUCKY FEUD

THE GREAT HATFIELD-McCOY DUELS

SHOWN IN MOVING PICTURES

Another Sensational Biograph Romance of the Order of the Famous "Moonshiners"

THE CAUSE OF THE FEUD

A Wonderful Production in Photography and Action

LENGTH 675 FEET, CLASS "A"

Produced and Controlled Exclusively by the

American Mutoscope & Biograph Co.

II East 14th Street, New York City.

A KENTUCKY FEUD

Inspired by the success of their motion picture THE MOONSHINER, AM&B undertook to document a bitter, real-life drama, the world-renowned feud between two Kentucky mountaineer families, the Hatfields and the McCoys. When completed, their film, entitled A KENTUCKY FEUD, ran approximately eight minutes and ended with a terrific knife duel to the death between the oldest sons of the Hatfield and McCoy clans. Not content with the usual inducements to buy the film, AM&B further intrigued prospective customers by saying in their handbill, "the last three scenes will be supplied, if desired, tinted for moonlight effect, and, as may readily be imagined, are of intense interest."

Made by the same company less than a year apart, both A KENTUCKY FEUD and THE MOONSHINER document violence, yet the camera technique differed greatly. To make A KENTUCKY FEUD, a camera was placed once for each scene to act as if it were a witness to an actual happening, whereas the feeling of violence was heightened for the audience by frequent camera movement during the filming of the earlier THE MOONSHINER.

A KENTUCKY FEUD, photographed in just one day at Sound Beach, Connecticut by Billy Bitzer, was copyrighted by AM&B on November 7, 1905. Descriptive titles preceded each of the eight episodes of the 285-foot film.

THE SILVER WEDDING

The title, THE SILVER WEDDING, would lead one to believe that the moving picture had largely to do with 25 years of wedded bliss. Instead, it is a film that, quoting AM&B's handbill, "shows the remarkable condition of affairs existing in New York City at the present day among the crooks and members of the underworld, exposing their methods of operation." Once more AM&B turned to an actual happening as a source for a motion picture.

THE SILVER WEDDING is about a cleverly organized and executed burglary of the presents given to a wealthy couple on their wedding anniversary. The culprits make their getaway down through the sewers of New York City where they are captured after a fierce struggle with the police. "The final scene, a positive novelty in moving pictures, shows the interior of one of the huge trunk-line sewers of the city," is one of the 25 lines of copy written in an attempt to convince exhibitors they should buy the film, copyrighted on March 8, 1906.

The man who designed and photographed this 264-foot production was F. A. Dobson. Very little is known about his career as a cameraman, but, judging from his work at AM&B, he was as advanced in the field of motion picture-making as any of his contemporaries, and he evidently believed that there was drama in the everyday walks of life that could be captured by a moving picture camera. In THE SILVER WEDDING, Dobson made use of cross lighting to add to the somberness of the scene when he filmed the action in the set built to resemble the sewer line. Dobson moved the camera many times throughout the film.

The Black Hand

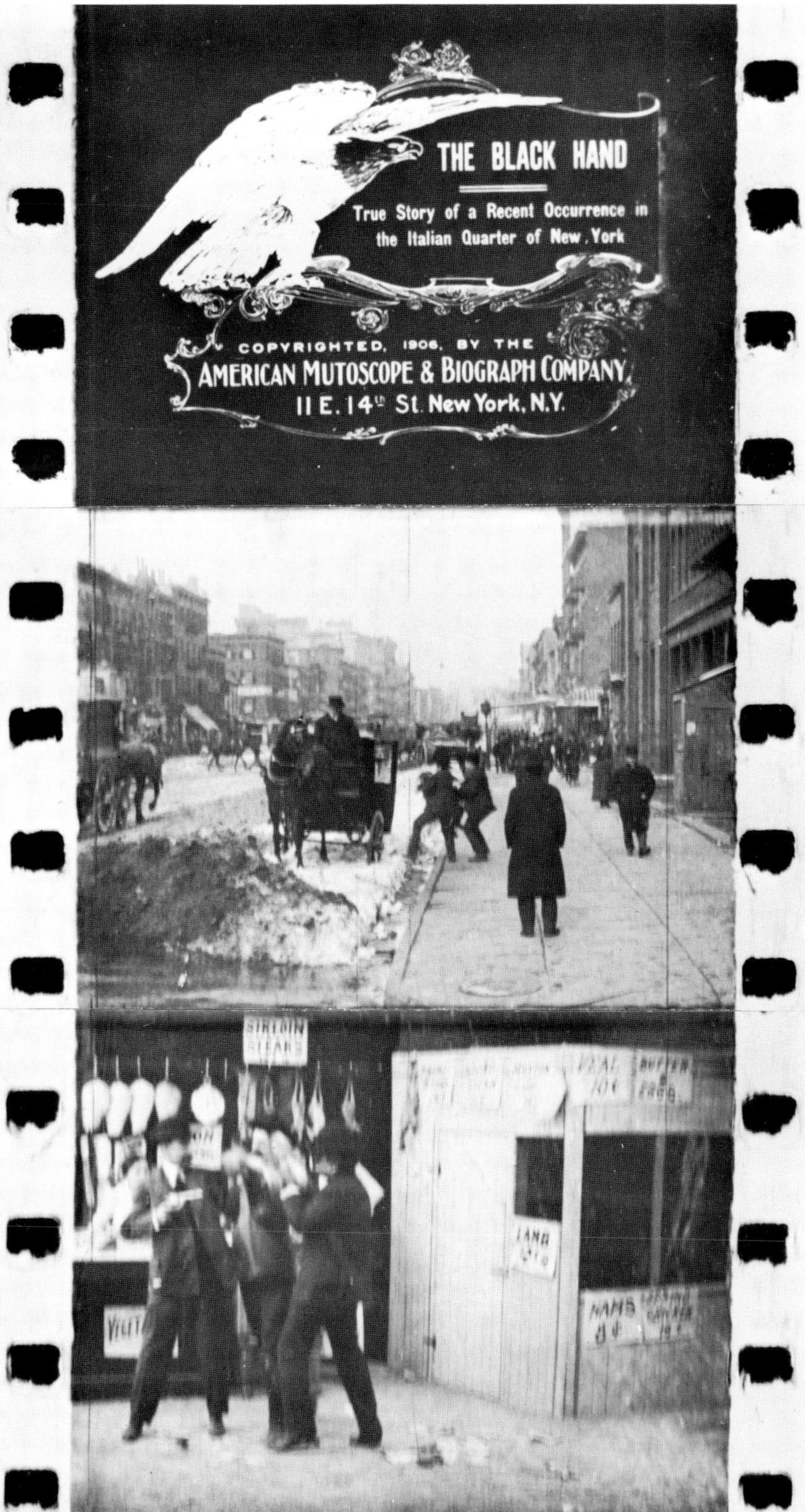

THE BLACK HAND

In the same month as THE SILVER WEDDING, AM&B once more turned to the police files as a source of inspiration for a motion picture. The result, THE BLACK HAND, is a film documentation of a dramatic kidnapping that occurred in New York City.

The opening title of the film, "True story of a recent occurrence in the Italian quarter of New York," gives no indication that the story line of the motion picture is of the kidnapping of a little girl by the notorious Black Hand society. They attempt to extort $1,000 from her parents by threatening to kill her. The blackmailers are eventually captured by the police who wait, teeth chattering, in an icebox for the abductors to appear to collect the ransom money.

Again carefully worded titles were employed to explain each forthcoming scene. In the opening episode of this 269-foot film, there was a two-shot that changed to a tight closeup insert to dramatize the warning note from the Black Hand group. Billy Bitzer photographed the exteriors on Seventh Avenue in New York City, and spectators in the background in the film watching him work seem transfixed. THE BLACK HAND was copyrighted by AM&B on March 24, 1906.

FORM NO. 1222   BULLETIN No. 72, June 28, 1906

THE PAYMASTER

Romance of Life in a New England Mill Town

LENGTH 685 FEET, PRICE 12 CENTS PER FOOT.

In "THE PAYMASTER" we have endeavored to give to moving pictures what "The Homestead" and "Shore Acres" are to the stage, a drama of homely American life, true to nature in all its details. In order to accomplish this our work was done in a New England village, centering in a big woolen mill, in which works the heroine, a pretty mill-girl. She loves the manly young paymaster of the mill, and he honestly loves her. The superintendent, a double-dyed villain, seeks to come between them, and failing in this, endeavors to ruin the paymaster by stealing the payroll and accusing the paymaster of the crime. His villainy is revealed by a dog who leads the heroine to the spot where the stolen money has been buried on the river bank. The girl confronts the dastardly superintendent with his crime, and he hurls her into the mill-pond above the falls. She is rescued in the nick of time by the hero, and the villain gets his just reward. The scenes are as follows: The Birthday Fete; In the Mill, showing the girl at work at the looms, an actual scene; The Conspiracy; The Robbery of the Payroll; Riot of the Mill-hands; The Burial of the Money, by Moonlight (tinted); The Dog Detective and the Recovery of the Money; The Denouement and the Daring Rescue at the Mill-pond.

Produced and Controlled Exclusively by the

American Mutoscope & Biograph Co.

11 East 14th Street, New York City.

PACIFIC COAST BRANCH, 2623 West Pico Street, Los Angeles, Cal.

THE PAYMASTER

Painted motion picture sets had so little dimension that film-makers sometimes travelled great distances to photograph in surroundings that would lend authenticity to their films, as well as eliminate the cost of building sets. AM&B had discovered an abandoned woolen mill with a still-operable millrace and waterfall in a picturesque spot in Sound Beach, Connecticut, and they took their motion picture company there to film still another true story, THE PAYMASTER.

The story line of the motion picture is built around a mill superintendent who plans and executes a payroll robbery in order to discredit the paymaster and get his girl. The film begins with a closeup of the paymaster—hero as he counts the payroll. Several episodes later, after the robbery, there are scenes of the burial and discovery of the stolen money. These were photographed during the day, but, in order to convey the impression of moonlight, the scenes were tinted or dyed by hand, not done on the paper roll sent to Washington for copyright.

THE PAYMASTER marks the debut in films of Gene Gauntier, the young lady who plays the mill girl, who went on to become one of the better-known motion picture actresses of the period. In her autobiography, Miss Gauntier says she was promised $3 for the day's work, which included being thrown into the millstream fully clothed. Her acting pleased the management so much, especially after it was discovered that she didn't know how to swim, that she was given $5.

This 274-foot motion picture was copyrighted by AM&B on June 23, 1906. The part of the hero was played by Gordon Burby; the villain was Jim Slevin. Billy Bitzer was the cameraman, and a Mr. Harrington has been credited with the direction.

THE TUNNEL WORKERS

Study of the many films made between 1898 and 1907 discloses that the principal subject was comedy, usually with a chase. Occasionally, however, there were outstanding exceptions to the comedy rule, such as THE TUNNEL WORKERS and THE SKY-SCRAPERS, two motion pictures based on current happenings. Made less than a month apart, both were photographed by F. A. Dobson, who had also filmed THE SILVER WEDDING just a few months earlier. Dobson had been with AM&B for eight years at the time he photographed these motion pictures for them.

Judging by these two films and others that he made, Dobson enjoyed photographing little-known dangerous jobs, bringing to light with a motion picture camera the occupational hazards involved. He then wove a plausible, understandable story with which the audience could identify around the filmed action.

Dobson photographed much of THE TUNNEL WORKERS on actual location, and film of crews changing shifts was used for the background of a drama that involved a triangle between a foreman and his wife and the project superintendent.

For the dramatic fight scene, Dobson built another excellent set, a most believable replica of an airlock of the tunnel and had an explosion occur during the fight. The effect of the explosion and the rescue of the men was increased by camera movement—something that Dobson seemed to understand a little ahead of most of his colleagues. The intensity of the light was also varied to bring more dramatic value to scenes.

AM&B copyrighted the 330-foot-long THE TUNNEL WORKERS on November 10, 1906. Jim Slevin has the role of the superintendent, while Guy Hedlund plays the part of the wronged husband, with Kate Toncray as the wife.

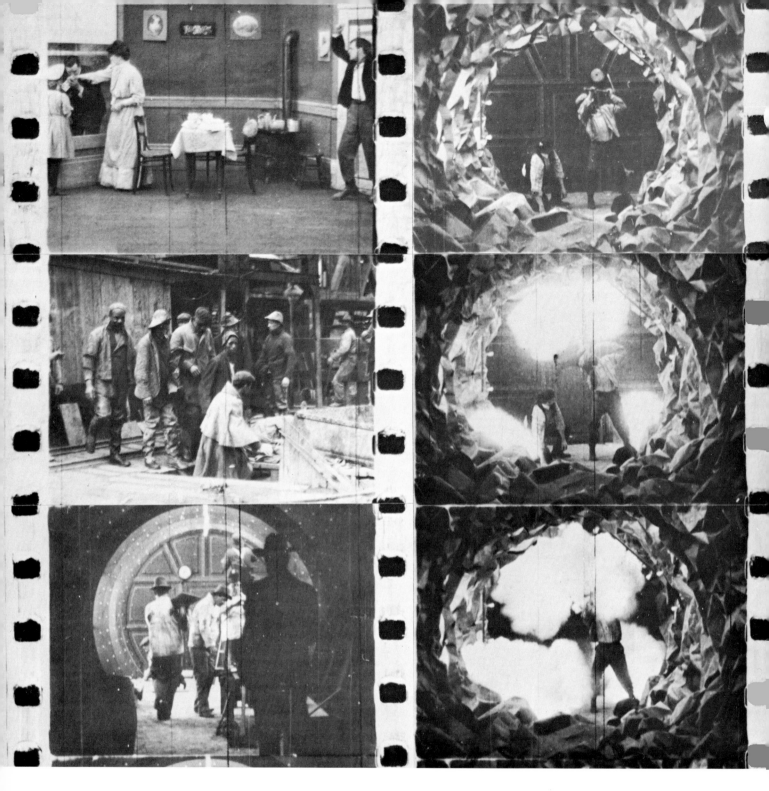

THE SKYSCRAPERS

Another hazardous occupation in major cities at the beginning of the century was constructing steel framework for skyscrapers, and again F. A. Dobson took his camera to the scene to document the various phases of this dangerous work. The result, a film called THE SKYSCRAPERS, is a story of the attempts of a disgruntled construction worker to discredit his foreman by framing him for theft. The conflict is combined with actual construction of the building as the work is in progress. There is even one scene of a hand-to-hand fight between the foreman and the construction worker that takes place on the unprotected ledge of the steel framework of the building. For this scene, Dobson created an effect of height and danger by photographing a long pan of the city, besides showing the men at work as they riveted large steel girders while their fellow workers scrambled about in the background high above the streets.

By photographing the fight scene from a lower position, F. A. Dobson was able to increase the effect of height and danger. Then, by raising his camera above the rescue scene, he duplicated the impression.

THE SKYSCRAPERS was photographed near Union Square in New York City, and some of the buildings that made New York's skyline world-famous can be seen. Jim Slevin and Gene Gauntier are among the cast. The film was 284 feet in length and was copyrighted by AM&B on December 11, 1906.

MR. HURRY-UP OF NEW YORK
THE TIRED TAILOR'S DREAM

We have tried to discuss films in the order of their copyright dates but MR. HURRY-UP OF NEW YORK and THE TIRED TAILOR'S DREAM are a deviation from that policy because, in common, they represent a complete departure from the usual type of film produced in the early years of motion picture-making, as well as being unique contributions to communication through that medium.

It is surprising that such expensive to produce films as these two were made as late as 1907 by any studio. The attitude of all producers was why take a week to make a film when one could be produced in a day or two that would immediately start making money for them.

They had also discovered that making films out of doors was not only easier and less expensive for them but also that the photographic results were far more satisfactory. Instead of having to construct costly sets, their cameramen could photograph against existing buildings and take advantage of anything interesting that happened to be going on, rather than have to bear the expense of bringing the outside world to the studio. In addition, the slow film manufactured at the time gave better results when it could be exposed in the sun rather than under the inadequate studio lighting that was all that was available to early motion picture-makers. Poor lighting increased the contrast of orthochromatic film and decreased the modeling of the subjects.

More than ten constructed sets were necessary in order to film MR. HURRY-UP OF NEW YORK, a delightful spoof on the supposed speed at which all New Yorkers conduct their lives. In the film, the businessman-hero rushes to dress, to eat, to work, to the dentist, and then to a saloon to drink away the pain. His inebriation sets the stage for the use of trick effects that begin with his attempt to put a flexible key into a wandering keyhole. His apparent bewilderment at his lack of success in opening the door is a highly amusing scene.

When the besotted businessman finally gets into his home, furniture begins to move, appear and disappear, and a circular staircase revolves, creating a dilemma for our hero when he tries to mount it. A camera was positioned above the set where the hero is sleeping in a drunken stupor to show the bed spinning on its axis, then defying gravity and taking off into the air.

By the time the 265-foot film was completed, most of the special camera effects known at the time had been employed in a moving picture that must have exceeded a week in production time. The paper copy of the film shows that some of the trick effects were accomplished by editing and splicing rather than by stop camera action.

Billy Bitzer photographed MR. HURRY-UP OF NEW YORK for AM&B who copyrighted it on January 31, 1907.

THE TIRED TAILOR'S DREAM

The expense of making THE TIRED TAILOR'S DREAM would be inestimable by today's standards. It is a filmed story of a man's suit being tailored completely by automatic means. The bolt of material unrolls itself, the chalk and triangle make the markings, the scissors cuts the material, the suit assembles itself and is stitched on a sewing machine, all without visible human aid. For instance, the camera had to be stopped and started a minimum of a hundred times in order to properly film the scissors as it cut the material. This was an exacting, time-consuming task and, even with today's equipment, such a scene would take at least two days to film.

The combination of stopping and starting the camera, coupled with "flying" the articles that moved, is perhaps the earliest example of this motion picture-making technique in the

Library of Congress paper print collection. Flying articles that moved and dressing the actor was accomplished by the use of threads and a puppeteer's yoke. Forty years later this same method made the "Topper" series a sensation in motion pictures, and after that on television. The entire film was photographed on one set from one camera position, although lenses of two different millimeters and focal lengths were used. There is also a dissolve made in a printer in this moving picture.

THE TIRED TAILOR'S DREAM, 245 feet in length, was copyrighted by AM&B on August 27, 1907. Photographed by the versatile F. A. Dobson, the film is another and entirely different example of his work as a cameraman. Dobson worked for AM&B from 1898 through 1907, a period of nine years. By 1915, he was out in Hollywood working for the LK-O studios.

112

WILLIAM N. SELIG

The fantastic profits that could be made from motion pictures naturally attracted a wide variety of persons to the industry, one of whom was a former minstrel showman, William N. Selig of Chicago, who became intrigued with its possibilities about 1896. Once Selig discovered that films about cowboys, Indians, and animals were consistent money-makers, he made a career of specializing in them.

THE GIRL FROM MONTANA
HIS FIRST RIDE
THE BANDIT KING

The Girl From Montana

Three of the earliest films with a story line ever made in California were Selig's THE GIRL FROM MONTANA, HIS FIRST RIDE, and THE BANDIT KING. All were photographed in a period of 30 days in and around Los Angeles in 1907 when the Selig company made an exploratory trip seeking a new studio location. It has been rumored that Selig's travels to California were largely motivated by his need to flee Chicago and the Edison process servers, something that was not uncommon for independent motion picture people in those days. Whatever Selig's reason, within four years after his arrival in California, profits from these three little films and others just like them, enabled him to build a studio in Los Angeles that exceeded in grandeur any other in the United States.

THE GIRL FROM MONTANA

THE GIRL FROM MONTANA is a Western with a twist. The hero is a heroine who ultimately saves her boy friend from being unjustly hanged by the bad guys. The cowgirl simply rides past the proceedings and shoots the rope off his neck just in time. The picture was 49 feet long and was copyrighted by William N. Selig on March 14, 1907.

HIS FIRST RIDE

The 21-foot epic of a runaway bicycle and a tyro rider called HIS FIRST RIDE has a different approach to film-making than the Selig Company's usual shoot'em-up Western. The film shows a great deal more pre-production thinking than either of the other two Selig films. The director applied the incidents of a chase sequence without the customary accumulation of a raggle-taggle group following the offender down the street. The extremely short film is made up of several different scenes of the unskilled bicycle rider passing the camera position each time as he gets himself into different and ridiculous situations, such as knocking down a man, an old woman with some laundry, etc. The copyright date is March 29, 1907.

The Bandit King

THE BANDIT KING

Another Western is Selig's THE BANDIT KING that starts off with a bank robbery. The cowboy actors are seen as they emerge from a building blown open by dynamite. The remaining scenes are vignettes that are so short that projection speed gives the illusion of a series of still photographs. The individual scenes are: blowing up a strong box, hold-up of a stagecoach, robbery of another bank, reporting the robbery to the sheriff, summoning the posse, the chase, capture, and killing of the bandits, and return of loot to its owners—all in 25 feet! Copyright date is April 11, 1907.

It is difficult to comment on the photographic quality of these three Selig pictures as the paper rolls that were sent for copyright were in such condition that they did not reproduce very well. The exact number of motion pictures made by William N. Selig prior to 1908 is not known, but he did send 16 paper rolls to the Library of Congress for copyright purposes between 1903 and 1908, only 12 of which are still available for viewing.

The Coming Of Columbus

After Pope Pius X recommended that Catholics not attend motion pictures, William N. Selig made a film early in 1912 called THE COMING OF COLUMBUS, with Charles Clary as Columbus, and Kathlyn Williams as Queen Isabella. When Selig looked around for ships to represent the caravels of Columbus, he learned that replicas presented by Spain to the United States at the time of the World's Columbian Exposition in Chicago in 1893 were still at anchor in a park lake in Chicago, a circumstance that saved him much trouble and expense. Selig presented a hand-tinted copy of THE COMING OF COLUMBUS to the Pope and was awarded a medal for elevating the moral standards of the motion picture industry. The medal is now on permanent exhibit at the Academy of Motion Picture Arts & Sciences in Hollywood.

Selig had become one of America's largest producer-distributors by 1925. Nevertheless, he died in relative obscurity in Hollywood on July 16, 1948. He had not had any connection with the motion picture business since about 1925.

AN ARCADIAN ELOPEMENT

Today communicating with a film audience is simple compared with early silent movies, as now there is the added element of sound. Sometimes titles preceded each scene in early films to provide a clue as to what was about to happen; the picture soon became uninteresting unless there was a great deal of activity. One of the ways pioneer directors coped with the problem was to speed up the action by having a chase sequence somewhere in the film, and by 1907 this type of film had become so popular and made so much money for producers that it became standard procedure to include a chase sequence in nearly every picture, whether it had any connection with the plot or not.

An example of this is AM&B's motion picture, AN ARCADIAN ELOPEMENT, advertised and copyrighted on September 16, 1907, as AN ACADIAN ELOPEMENT. The story line of this film is of a young couple who elope and begin their honeymoon, during which the irritating, pugnacious groom proceeds to have an altercation with every individual he encounters. Finally, he makes the mistake of disparaging some clam diggers at work, who throw him bodily into the water. Instead of ending the picture there, the producers added a scene of an escaped lunatic who disturbs the honeymooners as they stroll in lover's lane. This chase sequence made absolutely no contribution to the film, other than to lengthen it.

Even though the first film title indicates that the picture was photographed at a marriage mill in Nova Scotia, it actually was photographed in Portsmouth and Rye Beach, resort cities on the coast of New Hampshire by A. L. Poore and O. M. Gove. They were staff photographers who traveled as far afield as California to supply scenic films for AM&B's Mutoscope viewing device. By 1914, O. M. Gove was photographing pictures in Santa Monica for the Kalem Company. AN ARCADIAN ELOPEMENT is 312 feet long.

THE BOY DETECTIVE

Wallace McCutcheon, AM&B's head film director, concluded that if a serial story sold newspapers, a filmed series based on the same character undoubtedly would sell motion pictures. For this experiment, he chose a current newspaper serial character known as "Swipsey," whose filmed exploits were first recorded in THE BOY DETECTIVE.

In the motion picture, Swipsey, a newspaper boy-detective, foiled two would-be abductors of a wealthy broker's daughter. Swipsey accomplished this astounding feat by dressing in the young woman's clothing and taking her place in her carriage. When the abduction was attempted, Swipsey held the criminals at bay with a pistol until the police arrived.

This 90-foot film was photographed from ten different camera positions. In order to provide a dramatic ending for the story, McCutcheon, the director, had his cameraman, Billy Bitzer, move the camera in for a waist closeup of the hero, so that the audience would realize that the weapon he used was nothing more than a novelty cigarette case in the shape of a revolver.

The part of Swipsey was played by a girl, while "Swifty," the messenger boy, was played by Robert Harron. THE BOY DETECTIVE was copyrighted by AM&B on March 7, 1908.

TRADE **AB** MARK

The trademark of an A and B combined in a circle that was becoming so well known with the increasing popularity of AM&B motion pictures made a very obvious debut in HER FIRST ADVENTURE. At this time, plaigarism as well as outright theft were running rampant. Some independent distributors had even gone so far as to remove the beginning and ending titles from motion pictures, substituting their own, and selling the films as their own product. True, there were existing laws against such activities, but the means to enforce such laws was a completely different story. By the time an injured motion picture producer resorted to a civil lawsuit, the only means of redress available to him, the picture in question had made the rounds and had lost its box office appeal and most of its earning power.

Placement of a trademark in each scene to make it impossible for the unscrupulous to disguise the true producer of the film was about his only recourse.

The use of a trademark in at least one or more scenes of a motion picture was not original with AM&B, but dates back at least as far as Edison's THE LIFE OF AN AMERICAN FIREMAN. After employing the AB trademark in HER FIRST ADVENTURE, AM&B continued to use this symbol in every one of their next 400 motion pictures.

HER FIRST ADVENTURE

In 1905 the American Mutoscope & Biograph Company imported and copyrighted one of England's earliest and most popular film productions, RESCUED BY ROVER, already mentioned in this book. Three years later, AM&B made their version of this film and called it HER FIRST ADVENTURE. Instead of an infant being kidnapped by gypsies, however, AM&B's moving picture was the tale of a little girl who became so enchanted with the music of a hurdy gurdy and the gypsy couple who accompanied it that she followed them all around town until she became lost. When the little girl's parents missed her, they sent Rover, her collie dog, to search for her. Suspense was built up when director Wallace McCutcheon made it plain that the child and her new-found acquaintances were wandering further and further from home. In order to heighten the anxiety and suspense during the search, McCutcheon cut back from time to time to show the faithful Rover diligently combing the countryside for his small mistress.

In the last scene in the picture, after the child is found, the camera moves from the rejoicing rescue group in for a tight head-and-shoulder closeup of Rover.

HER FIRST ADVENTURE, 201 feet long, was copyrighted by AM&B on March 13, 1908 and was photographed by Billy Bitzer in a small New Jersey town.

FORM NO. 1301   BULLETIN No. 129, March 21, 1908.

CAUGHT BY WIRELESS

The Efficacy of the Marconigram Shown in Motion Pictures

LENGTH, 969 FEET.   **PRICE, 14 CENTS PER FOOT.**

MARCONI STATION ON AN OCEAN LINER

Routed out of the groove of conventionality, the Biograph Company presents a thrilling dramatic story, that is as novel as it is interesting, based on the egregious possibilities of wireless telegraphy. The opening scenes are laid in Ireland, the first showing the interior of an Irish cabin, at which a despotic land agent calls to collect rent. Finding the husband absent, offers insult to the wife. The timely arrival of the husband results in the thrashing of the agent. The agent swears vengeance and returns later with two policemen, to arrest the husband, but the trio gets a warm reception, and in the skirmish, the husband escapes and is advised later by a friend to leave the country which he does, after a tearful adieu to his wife and children. He takes the first steamer to America.

The land agent proves himself an unconscionable villain, who not only casts aside his faithful wife, but two years later burglarizes his employer's safe and flees unintercepted on a liner bound for New York. He would have made good his escape but for the mercurial celerity of the Marconi contrivance, with which the ship was provided. From Scotland Yard, London, a message for his apprehension is flashed to the steamer, which is in turn flashed to the New York police headquarters.

Fortuitously, on the same boat there are as passengers, the wife and children of the young Irishman, who having succeeded in getting appointed on the police force of New York, had sent for his dear ones to join him. The villain is recognized by the wife while on the ship, so of course his capture is an easy matter when the boat touched the dock at New York, where the happy reunited family have the satisfaction of seeing their persecutor run to earth.

The film is replete with stirring situations of a thrillingly sensational character, and the Marconi device, which is accurately reproduced, is most interesting and novel.

No. 3394   **CODE WORD—Reveleras.**

CAUGHT BY WIRELESS

By the time AM&B produced CAUGHT BY WIRELESS in March of 1908, motion picture projection was entering its second decade, and with it a pattern of production and distribution began to emerge. Trade magazines containing ads of the various licensed film-producing companies were available in every state in the Union. Each producer named a specific day of the week that his films could be seen in the neighborhood theaters, and audiences looked forward to their favorite evening at the movies. AM&B started out with a new release every Friday and were now proudly announcing that, "our films run on any machine," proving that they now had converted to the 35mm film width used by the rest of the motion picture world. The price of AM&B's prints had risen from 12 to 14c a foot.

One thing that did remain constant, however, was the search for novelty in stories that could be released in a ten-minute reel of film. The recent perfection of ship-to-shore communication via the Marconi wireless suggested the plot of CAUGHT BY WIRELESS to someone at AM&B. It was such an innovation to actually be able to see a Marconi wireless in operation that the executives at AM&B, as a possible box office lure, said in their handbill, "the Marconi device, which is accurately reproduced, is most interesting and novel." CAUGHT BY WIRELESS is a 370-foot drama that starts in Ireland and ends in the United States. The high point of the story is the capture of a fugitive made possible when the authorities in New York are notified by wireless of the name of the ship on which the villain was fleeing from Ireland. CAUGHT BY WIRELESS is still another instance of a motion picture based on an actual happening.

The direction of CAUGHT BY WIRELESS was supervised by Wallace McCutcheon. Billy Bitzer was the cameraman, and the film was copyrighted by AM&B on March 18, 1908.

THE PRINCESS IN THE VASE

The association between David Wark Griffith and G. W. Billy Bitzer as a director-cameraman team earned them a reputation in the motion picture business unequalled by any other such combination. According to the records, they made in excess of 300 motion pictures together before they left AM&B in 1913. The date they met is not known, but Griffith did appear as a principal actor in a movie that took the first two weeks of February 1908 to complete called THE PRINCESS IN THE VASE. The photographic credit was shared between Bitzer and Arthur Marvin. The film is a complicated comedy involving trick photography. The action of the picture is aided by a cutback, the drama by a scene beginning in total darkness, and stop motion special effects photography adds excitement. In one scene, the camera was run backwards to give the illusion that smoke is going back into a vase. THE PRINCESS IN THE VASE, 364 feet long, was copyrighted by AM&B on February 25, 1908.

D. W. Griffith as an actor in Roman costume in two scenes from "Princess in the Vase."

THE SCULPTOR'S NIGHTMARE

Two months and several motion pictures later, Bitzer photographed another trick film, THE SCULPTOR'S NIGHTMARE, in which Griffith again had a role as an actor, this time as part of a crowd.

Man on extreme right is D. W. Griffith in
THE SCULPTOR'S NIGHTMARE.

THE SCULPTOR'S NIGHTMARE, a film with political overtones, used a story with actors to set the stage for the creation by a sculptor of plaster busts of such major political luminaries of the era as Teddy Roosevelt, Charles W. Fairbanks, William H. Taft, and William Jennings Bryan, as well as a Teddy bear, and the G.O.P. elephant.

To make the various clay figures grow before the eyes of the film audience, the following procedure was used. The sculptor worked at his modeling for a pre-determined period of time. A few frames of film were photographed, one frame at a time, and the sculptor then continued until the modeling was completed. A few years earlier, Edwin S. Porter had photographed a film called FUN IN A BAKERY SHOP, also discussed in this book. For that motion picture, Porter used time lapse photography while the sculptor was at work, but in THE SCULPTOR'S NIGHTMARE, Bitzer used stop motion with the sculptor not seen at any time, as he wanted to provide the illusion that the busts were being sculptured without human aid. The finished statues in THE SCULPTOR'S NIGHTMARE were animated and performed such actions as smoking a cigar, laughing, etc., while the busts in the Edison picture remained inanimate.

The clay models were signed by Barkman. Also in the large cast of THE SCULPTOR'S NIGHTMARE was Mack Sennett, in what probably was his earliest appearance in an AM&B motion picture. The film has a copyright date of May 4, 1908 and is 266 feet long.

THE SCULPTOR'S NIGHTMARE — man seated in center is Mack Sennett.

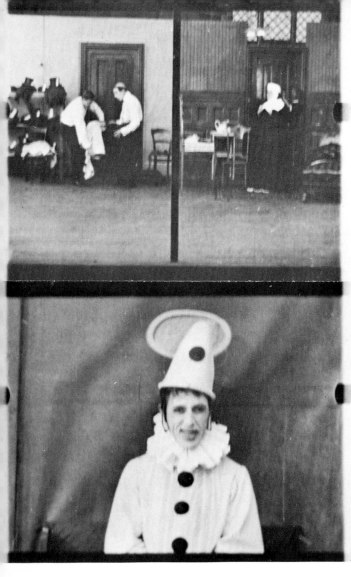

AT THE FRENCH BALL.
Man in upper left picture and
at bottom is D. W. Griffith.

AT THE FRENCH BALL

From January of 1908 until AT THE FRENCH BALL was made in June of the same year, D. W. Griffith was busy acting in approximately one one-reel AM&B feature per week. ADVENTURES OF DOLLIE, his first directorial assignment, was yet to come.

AT THE FRENCH BALL is a comedy about a husband, played by Griffith, and wife, who are caught in the toils of their own deceit when both attend the same masquerade ball in costume without telling the other, and each accidentally becomes aware of the other's true identity.

In AT THE FRENCH BALL, Bitzer brought to play the same split set idea that he had used in the 1905 production, THE GREAT JEWEL MYSTERY, of placing a timber vertically in such a position that it appeared to the camera as a wall dividing two rooms, thus permitting simultaneous independent action. In this way, the audience had an easier time following the story, less motion picture film was used, and a difficult problem of editing was eliminated.

In another scene, the director, Wallace McCutcheon, moved the camera in for a head-and-shoulder closeup of each of the principals, one of whom was Griffith. McCutcheon was aware even then that facial expressions do not show well on the screen if the camera is any distance from the actors.

It was not until about 1912 that names of motion picture actors began appearing on the screen and, because of the masks and costumes, the only two identified members of the cast are D. W. Griffith and Robert Harron.

AT THE FRENCH BALL is 247 feet long, and AM&B copyrighted it on June 20, 1908. Through some error, both paper rolls sent to the Library of Congress for copyright bore the incorrect title of OVER THE HILLS TO THE POORHOUSE, another AM&B production with the same copyright date.

BIOGRAPH/GRIFFITH ERA

It was with some trepidation that we approached the Biograph/Griffith era that began in 1908. After all, a great deal already had been written about D. W. Griffith and his work, and perhaps we wouldn't be able to contribute anything of significance. Then we compared the titles of the nearly 400 restored Griffith-directed Biograph films with those usually discussed and realized that the majority of that number, particularly the over 100 he made in his first year with that company, apparently never had been studied.

Many authors have rightfully lauded Griffith's talents and capabilities, but their opinions seem to have been based on the same few films for, until the paper print restoration program was completed, only a very small percentage of the films he directed was available in any one place for study purposes.

When we looked at and analyzed all of the restored Griffith motion pictures in order of copyright date, we found that we were watching the progress of a man who had been trained for the stage and his successful transition to a director of a new communication medium, an entirely new field for him. There was scarce precedent to guide him, and his sole preparation for the motion picture field had been as an actor in about two dozen films. Nevertheless, his earliest motion pictures show almost from the first he was able to visualize an entire moving picture before it was photographed and then transfer that idea to the screen in such a way that it became a box office success.

The American Mutoscope & Biograph Company was barely meeting its competition when they left the independent producing field in 1908 to become part of the Motion Picture Patents Company, a move which gave them a considerably larger market for their film product. As Gene Gauntier, in the script department of the AM&B studio at the time, says in her autobiography:

"Griffith's entry as director was most opportune for in a few weeks Biograph gave up its fight against the Motion Picture Patents Company and entered the fold. This had been a losing fight and had reduced the company to financial straits. I doubt very much whether Griffith would have had such a swift success had they remained independent, in spite of the fact that his pictures began immediately to create a furore. As an independent, Biograph had been selling but 10 or 12 copies of each picture. Now with a sure market and a director acclaimed as great, their sales quickly surpassed all others. Before long, it was not uncommon for them to sell a hundred copies of each production."

It was difficult to limit ourselves to only 16 motion pictures from Griffith's formative period as a director, but we think that each motion picture selected reveals another facet of his ability as a film-maker. While all are representative of his work, they leave the door slightly ajar to the many others he made that are now available for study.

The few motion picture companies of that era were well aware that the best way to hold the interest of an audience was to give them something to laugh at or to ridicule unless, of course, the film was about a current event. Most of the films made in the first ten years of production were comedies. At first, films were short, limited by the capacity of peephole viewing devices, and were usually climaxed by one person pouring some unattractive substance out of a bucket onto another person's head. Then along came projection and with it came the chase as a means to hold the attention of the audience for a longer period of time.

Drama was attempted, of course, but often it fell short in entertainment value because the technique of acting before a motion picture camera had not been sufficiently developed to convey a story line. The same gestures that were suitable for a dramatic situation on the stage when accompanied by speech merely made actors appear ridiculous on the silent screen. Audiences could not take dramatic pictures seriously and generally laughed at them. So producers had little choice but to continue making more comedies than dramas, but they were continually on the alert for some new gimmick around which to build the pratfall, the spilled bucket, or the chase.

A CALAMITOUS ELOPEMENT

Records show that in the first 60 days that Griffith worked for AM&B as a director of motion pictures, he maintained an incredible work schedule and completed 20 films during that time. When he made the slapstick comedy, A CALAMITOUS ELOPEMENT, he had been a director for less than 30 days and had made more than ten films, of which this was the eighth.

A CALAMITOUS ELOPEMENT is about a young, newlywed couple whose apartment was burglarized by a man who hid in their trunk when it was left unattended on the sidewalk. The trunk was carried into their apartment by a porter and an unwitting policeman, played by D. W. Griffith. When all was clear, the burglar emerged from the trunk, stole everything in sight, and went on his way.

Arthur Marvin and Billy Bitzer shared the photographic credit on A CALAMITOUS ELOPEMENT. The general impression is that Bitzer photographed all of the pictures directed by D. W. Griffith, but records show that of the first 20, Arthur Marvin, brother of one of the founders of AM&B, was the principal photographer with an occasional assist from Bitzer. Arthur Marvin was drowned in the tragic sinking of the "Titanic" in 1912. All of the outdoor scenes of A CALAMITOUS ELOPEMENT were taken in front of a building, the Biograph motion picture studio, a former private residence, at 11 East 14th Street in New York City.

The leading lady in A CALAMITOUS ELOPEMENT was Linda Arvidson, a former stage actress, then married to Griffith. They had agreed to keep their marriage a secret so that both could find employment in the strange new world of motion pictures. In addition to the above, John Cumpson, Tony O'Sullivan, and Frank Gebhardt also appear in the picture. D. W. Griffith, although now a director, filled out the cast, a not uncommon practice for him in his first films.

The copyright date of the 274-foot A CALAMITOUS ELOPEMENT is July 28, 1908.

Man in policeman's uniform is D. W. Griffith

BALKED AT THE ALTAR

Writers over the past 50 years seem to concentrate on D. W. Griffith's talent as a director of drama. Rarely does anyone mention his not inconsiderable ability as a director of comedy, although the paper print restoration program unearthed many delightful examples of his work in this field. In the early stages of Griffith's motion picture career, he was confronted with the same dilemma as all other directors of his time—what kind of a film should he make? He solved it by making many comedies in his first year as a director. As a matter of fact, AM&B's production requirement called for one one-reel drama and two split reels of comedy per week. A split reel is less than one-half the length of a 1,000-foot reel, or less than five minutes of running time.

One of the comedies that Griffith directed, BALKED AT THE ALTAR, his 13th picture, was a feature-length film photographed by Arthur Marvin, about a young lady who desperately wanted a husband. As a way to attract suitors, she sat outside her home reading a spicy best-selling novel by Elinor Glyn. This scheme worked so well she managed to get a suitor in front of the altar, with the aid of her father and his shotgun.

When the reluctant groom was asked to say yes, he bolted through the stained glass window of the church, running off through the streets of Fort Lee, New Jersey, pursued by all the wedding guests. Eventually dragged from a tree where he had taken refuge, the frightened groom was brought back to the church where he was confronted with the same question. This time he answered in the affirmative, but not so the bride-to-be, who haughtily stalked out of the church and returned home to her book. To accentuate the humor of the twist ending, D. W. Griffith moved the camera sufficiently close so that the movie audience could read the title "Three Weeks" of the book that the young lady found more exciting than getting married.

Mabel Stoughton in BALKED AT THE ALTAR

Among the cast of this motion picture are Harry Salter, Mabel Stoughton, Frank Gebhardt, Linda Arvidson, Arthur Johnson, and Mack Sennett. BALKED AT THE ALTAR was 276 feet long and was copyrighted by AM&B on August 15, 1908.

WHERE BREAKERS ROAR

In his second month as a director at AM&B, D. W. Griffith made his 21st film, WHERE BREAKERS ROAR, this time a drama. Griffith establishes the mood of the film by introducing his actors in a joyous, happy set of circumstances at a beach resort where they frolick in the sand. He then injects sinister drama into the film by cutting away from the beach fun to the front of an insane asylum where a struggle between a homicidal maniac and his guards is in progress. Griffith shows the maniac proceeding toward the beach, stopping only long enough to throttle a fisherman to steal his stiletto. The camera now shifts from the armed maniac to the beach where the heroine is intent on running away from her friends to escape a ducking. Griffith then shifts the scene back to the villain to show that he, also intent upon escape, is heading toward the same rowboat. They reach the boat simultaneously, and the maniac takes the girl hostage. The balance of the film is devoted to the capture of the maniac and her rescue. To prolong the suspense, and lengthen the scene, as well as to make the boat chase seem longer, Griffith placed the camera at different elevations on a pier and directed the pursued and the pursuers to row their boats past the camera position several times.

Linda Arvidson played the part of the young woman, with Arthur Johnson as her boy friend. Florence Lawrence, Mack Sennett, and Guy Hedlund were also in the cast. Harry Salter took the part of the villain, and the cameraman was Arthur Marvin. WHERE BREAKERS ROAR is 212 feet long and has a copyright date September 15, 1908.

Scenes from WHERE BREAKERS ROAR

AN AWFUL MOMENT

Whether the intent was to keep production cost down or whether film-makers of the Griffith era honestly felt that audiences would not accept a motion picture over one reel in length probably never will be known for certain. When we speak of Griffith's prodigious efforts in turning out many films in a short period of time, it must not be overlooked that each feature was one reel in length and lasted approximately ten minutes on the screen, depending upon the speed at which the projectionist cranked his machine. Nevertheless, when Griffith started as a director, he had to make a film that could be photographed in not more than two days, would be not more than one reel in length when completed, and would still hold the attention of an audience. To do this successfully must have required a great deal of pre-production planning on his part.

AN AWFUL MOMENT, made during Griffith's first six months as a director, is his 46th film. It tells the story of a vindictive gypsy's attempt to get revenge on a judge for a jail sentence. After leaving the court, the gypsy enters the judge's home, finds his wife asleep, and gives her gas. She then ties the judge's wife to a chair and arranges a shotgun with a string from its trigger to the doorknob, so that when the judge opens the door, he will trigger the gun and kill his wife. Fortunately, their small daughter awakens and removes the string from the doorknob just as the judge reaches for it.

In this film, Griffith again followed his pattern of setting a mood of tranquility and happiness, and then abruptly shattering it by showing this pleasant atmosphere about to be threatened. An unusual scene shows the judge as he unwraps a package inside a room while the face of the gypsy woman, bent on carrying out her threat against him, appears between parted curtains, especially since it immediately follows an exterior shot of the gypsy climbing the trellis with a knife in her teeth. Griffith restores the tranquil mood of the film by showing the happy family around a Christmas tree. For the final scene, he moved the camera in for a tight three-shot to reveal their pleased expressions.

AN AWFUL MOMENT was photographed in the studio and on 14th Street by Arthur Marvin. In the cast are: Linda Arvidson, Florence Lawrence, Marion Leonard, Kate Bruce, Adele DeGarde, Dorothy Bernard, Mack Sennett, and Florence Barker. The film was 287 feet long and was copyrighted by AM&B on December 10, 1908.

THE BANK ROBBERY

From 1894 until the time this film was photographed in 1908, well over one hundred companies with odd-sounding names made one or two films and then went out of business. One of them was the Oklahoma Natural Mutoscene Company who produced and copyrighted a total of three motion pictures. Probably no other motion picture was ever spawned from such a unique set of circumstances as their first effort, THE BANK ROBBERY.

Three incidents, completely unrelated, contributed to its existence. Teddy Roosevelt, then president of the United States, wanted to prove a statement he once made to the effect that he had seen at a Rough Rider reunion a John Abernathy strangle wolves with his bare hands. Thinking his story was not believed, Roosevelt dispatched a cameraman, J. B. Kent, to Oklahoma to photograph the famed wolf hunter in action. Kent arrived in Cache, the nearest town to the Wichita National Preserve, where the film of the wolf hunt was to be taken. While he was making preliminary arrangements to film Abernathy in action, Kent met Al Jennings, a reformed bank robber, who also was in Cache stumping for election as governor of the territory. The town of Cache had a small cattleman's bank which several years before had been robbed by the notorious Jennings and his gang. After some talk, it was decided to postpone filming the wolf hunt and to re-enact the bank robbery, with Al Jennings as star, Kent to photograph it, and William M. Tilghman, famous frontier marshal, as director. Jennings and Kent were experienced in their jobs but Tilghman's only qualification as a director, said his biographer, was that he always seemed to get things done.

The group began the moving picture with the bank robbery scene and developed the plot as they went along. According to Mrs. Tilghman's book, "Marshal of the Last Frontier," "..the film as finally worked out included a holdup of the bank at the little town of Cache, by Al Jennings and his gang. This was staged just at the close of business, by agreement with the banker. But a citizen who was present, and not 'in the know' jumped out of the window and ran to give the alarm, adding a bit of excitement that was entirely real."

The paper rolls from which the film THE BANK ROBBERY was restored show that two different cameras were used to photograph the picture. Apparently one was operated by an untrained man who became so enthralled over his job that when he was following the scene of the bank robbers leaving town he continued to pan the camera for almost 180 degrees so the picture includes a great number of persons standing on the wooden sidewalks in front of the town's business section obviously engrossed in watching the film being made.

The picture included not only the bank robbery but also the chase by the posse that ended in the inevitable shoot-out and capture of the robbers. The last scene in the film shows the remaining live bank robbers, handcuffed and bandaged, riding by the camera position, with Marshal Tilghman escorting Al Jennings, just as he had in real life.

THE BANK ROBBERY was photographed in Cache and in the Wichita National Preserve and is reputed to be the first time in film history that a reformed bank robber was asked to re-enact the actual occurrence for the benefit of a moving picture camera. Jennings' initial appearance in front of a camera so intrigued him that he tried to make a career out of acting after he was defeated in his campaign for governor. In 1915 he made WHEN OUTLAWS MEET, THE LADY OF THE DUGOUT, and was the subject of a filmed biography called BEATING BACK.

Date of copyright of THE BANK ROBBERY was December 28, 1908 and it was 692 feet long. The other two films made at the same time by the Oklahoma Natural Mutoscene Company were called THE WOLF HUNT, and A ROUND-UP IN OKLAHOMA, each a reel in length.

THE CORD OF LIFE

One of the most important compensations to come from viewing the restored films in the order they were made is that, for the first time, it is possible to see styles of photographic communication as each developed. Although other companies began making motion pictures as early as AM&B, it is remarkable that they were the sole company to send paper prints of their productions to the Copyright Office from their peep show days until it was no longer necessary for protection. But enough film made by other companies has survived for us to be able to make an honest comparison, and to know that all motion picture-makers of that era were confronted with identical growth problems. Therefore, AM&B can serve as a prototype for the embryonic motion picture industry.

In January of 1909 when Griffith began making THE CORD OF LIFE, he had been a director for less than eight months, and AM&B had released 62 of his films up to that time. Two of his earlier motion pictures, AN AWFUL MOMENT and WHERE BREAKERS ROAR, began in the spirit of happiness and were turned into suspense films later. But in THE CORD OF LIFE, Griffith immediately set the dramatic tone of the picture by having the villain suspend a basket containing the hero's baby outside a second-story window. He fiendishly attached a rope from basket to window in such a way that if the window were opened, baby would drop to the ground below. By putting this scene at the beginning of his film, Griffith made the audience aware of the baby's continuing peril.

The villain, not content with having placed the child's life in jeopardy, goes off to gloat over the father at the construction project where he works. Father immediately sets out for home, running across fields, and climbing fences, rushing to the aid of his endangered child. Griffith shows the audience his actor's anguished facial expression by directing him to run close by the camera. By today's standards, this would be a peculiar technique of film-making, but it was one early director's way of solving the problem of communicating with his audience. Nowadays, the same effect would be accomplished by a dolly shot.

While father rushes home, Griffith returns the audience to the interior of the apartment. Having already acquainted the audience with the baby's predicament and what could happen if someone opens the window, Griffith created incidents to cause mother to start for the window several times, as if to open it. On each occasion, she is prevented from such action by the timely arrival of someone at her door, the last time by her husband who, with much arm-waving, acquaints her with what has happened to the baby.

The Cord Of Life

Griffith used the chase technique combined with the cutback to the wife at home to prolong suspense as well as to make the audience think that father had a great distance to travel.

THE CORD OF LIFE was photographed by Arthur Marvin and Billy Bitzer in the New York studio and along the Palisades on the Hudson River in New Jersey. The film is 302 feet long and bears an AM&B copyright date of January 22, 1909. Among the cast are Charles Gorman, Marion Leonard, Guy Hedlund, Harry Salter, Linda Arvidson, Mack Sennett, John Cumpson, Charles French, Dorothy Bernard, and Clara T. Bracey, some of whom had very small parts.

THE GIRLS AND DADDY

Immediately following THE CORD OF LIFE, Griffith directed his 64th picture, a drama with still another approach, called THE GIRLS AND DADDY.

The film is the story of two young ladies who are observed by a burglar as they cash a money order in the post office. The burglar follows them home with the intention of stealing their money. Their happy chatter about plans to buy their father a gift is overheard by another man, a drunken sneak thief, who enters the house after the girls retire for the night, unaware that the burglar is already there. The drunken sneak thief makes so much noise as he ransacks the house that he awakens the girls, causing them to flee from their bedroom in terror.

The sneak thief follows and pursues them from room to room, battering down doors as he goes. Finally, the girls are cornered in the attic. One of them climbs a ladder to the roof to call for help. There she surprises the burglar just leaving with a bag full of loot. The young girl's terror is so sincere that the burglar goes to her aid, captures and holds the sneak thief until the police arrive.

From the moment the thief is discovered by the girls until his capture by the burglar, Griffith positioned and moved his camera five times. Each time the camera was so placed as to film both sides of the wall containing the door through which the frightened girls flee. The camera thus films the simultaneous action of the fearful girls as they attempt to hold the doors against the violence of the thief. In order to take full advantage of the facial expressions of his actors, Griffith placed his camera closer than usual to the action.

A good understanding of Griffith's method of directing was gained from study of the paper print of this film, because the paper roll was sent for copyright, not in the order it was finally edited, but as the 32 scenes originally were photographed and numbered. The paper roll shows that when Griffith placed the camera on a set or location, all of the action including retakes, regardless of continuity, was performed in front of the camera before it was moved to the next set. There was no camera movement in any scene. Nearly 2,500 35mm feet of film were used to photograph THE GIRLS AND DADDY, but that amount was edited down to 855 feet in the finished film. Marvin photographed 1,575 feet, while Bitzer filmed the remainder. It was photographed at Fort Lee, New Jersey and in the 14th Street studio.

Griffith quite often directed his actors and actresses to play more than one part. Clara T. Bracey plays a postal clerk in the beginning of the film, and turns up later in blackface. Her escort in that scene is Mack Sennett, whose second part in THE GIRLS AND DADDY was as one of the two policemen who made the arrest at the end of the film. Griffith also acted in THE GIRLS AND DADDY. Others were Florence Lawrence, Charles Inslee, Wilfred Lucas, Harry Salter, Dorothy Bernard, Arthur Johnson, Kate Bruce, Dorothy West, and Gladys Egan. The copyright date was February 3, 1909.

The enthusiastic spectator in blackface, checked coat, and derby hat to the left is D. W. Griffith, the director of THE GIRLS AND DADDY.

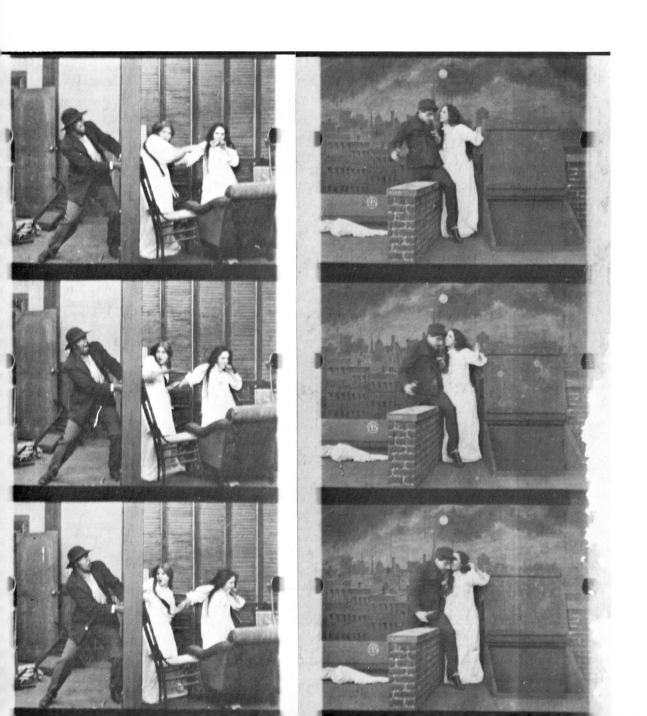

GOLDEN LOUIS
AT THE ALTAR

Almost from the very start of Griffith's career as a director, he seemed to understand how to make a motion picture that would hold the interest of an audience. Also, right from the beginning, he realized that moving a camera could bring elements to a motion picture that no amount of dialogue could bring to a stage play. Whether it was he who was responsible for camera movement in his first pictures is hard to say, for there are pictorial evidences of such camera uses in films photographed by his cameramen Marvin and Bitzer prior to his appointment as a director. As a matter of fact, Griffith, as an actor, is the subject of closeups in films photographed by both of these men before he became a director. Griffith knew the merits of camera movement, but seldom used it in his motion pictures unless he felt that such action could help to bring out a point in the story. Camera movement, such as the closeup, the close two-shot, matte shots, and other then uncommon camera uses are evident, however, in Griffith's first 75 motion pictures.

Two of his films, GOLDEN LOUIS and AT THE ALTAR, copyrighted a week apart, would completely lose their impact on the screen without camera movement.

The first, GOLDEN LOUIS, is the story of a little match girl. While she sleeps, a passerby gives her a coin, a golden louis, that later is stolen. Three times in the film, D. W. Griffith moved the camera in for a tight closeup of the coin, the first time as the coin was held in the hand of the donor, the second time in the child's wooden shoe, and the third time in the thief's hand. Without these three closeups, the audience would never have known a coin was involved.

Griffith moved his camera back and forth between the constructed sets of several street scenes, the steps on which the little match girl sleeps (and freezes to death), and the interior of a gambling casino, to strengthen the continuity of the film.

The part of the little match girl was taken by Gladys Egan. Also in the cast were Wilfred Lucas, Kate Bruce, Owen Moore, Mack Sennett, and Marion Leonard. The GOLDEN LOUIS was photographed in the studio by Arthur Marvin during D. W. Griffith's eighth month as a director at AM&B. The film was copyrighted on February 17, 1909 and was 181 feet long.

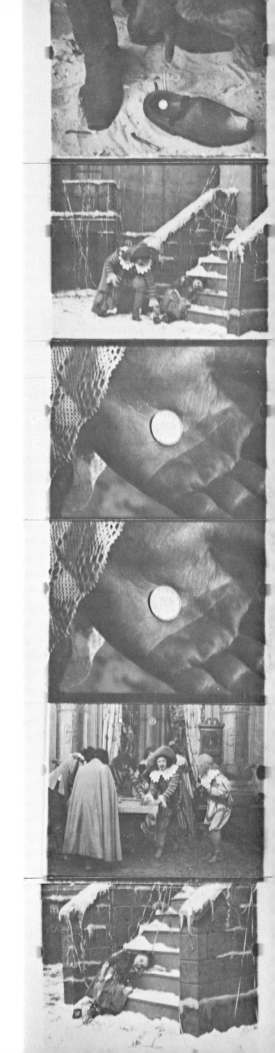

AT THE ALTAR

The same week that Griffith made the sentimental tragedy, GOLDEN LOUIS, he completed a suspense drama twice as long called AT THE ALTAR. The story is of a rejected suitor who, on learning that his girl intends to marry another, designs an infernal machine to kill his rival and the bride at the altar. He hides the weapon in the church and commits suicide. When the investigating policeman discovers the note left by the dead man, he realizes the impending danger and rushes off to the church to warn the couple.

Griffith adds suspense to the picture by alternating scenes of the policeman running through town with scenes of the wedding preliminaries, and increases tension by creating situations to impede the policeman's progress. After each obstacle, Griffith switches the scene to the church, keeping the audience aware how much closer the young couple are to death. When the policeman has almost reached his destination, he collapses from exhaustion. Griffith then moves the camera at least 100 yards, close enough to the fallen officer to show that he is unable to rise.

The scene again shifts to the interior of the church where the wedding is about to begin, with the bride and groom at the altar awaiting the arrival of the minister. The film ends as the policeman struggles to his feet just in time to prevent the minister from triggering the fatal device.

Arthur Marvin photographed AT THE ALTAR in Edgewater, New Jersey, and the 366-foot film was copyrighted on February 26, 1909.

Among the cast are Harry Salter, Marion Leonard, Linda Arvidson, John Cumpson, James Kirkwood, Florence Lawrence, Arthur Johnson, Kate Bruce, and Mack Sennett, who again had two parts. D. W. Griffith also appeared in one scene.

AT THE ALTAR

Mack Sennett, John Cumpson, Harry Salter, and
Marion Leonard in front row in first scene.

From left to right, Mack Sennett,
D. W. Griffith and Arthur Johnson.

Above, Harry Salter

SHE WOULD BE AN ACTRESS
DRUNKARD'S CHILD
AN UNEXPECTED GUEST

Unless company production records exist, there is little, if any, way to compare date of copyright of a film with the date it actually was made. If it were the general policy of an early film-making company to send a paper print of their productions off to Washington, then this was usually done as soon after completion of their films as possible.

The next three films, SHE WOULD BE AN ACTRESS, DRUNKARD'S CHILD, and AN UNEXPECTED GUEST, all were made by the Lubin Manufacturing Company of Philadelphia in 1909 and were copyrighted within a week of one another. Since Lubin was one of the companies that sent paper prints to Washington for copyright, it is safe to assume that these three pictures were made within a few days of one another, no small task for any film-maker, anywhere in the world, in 1909. However, records show that the Lubin Manufacturing Company applied for copyright on 103 films that same year, an average of two features a week. Of that number, paper rolls for only 18 titles have survived and have been restored. A study of the few that are available shows that the ability of Lubin and his associates as film-makers has been greatly underrated. Even from the few Siegmund Lubin films that are left from that era, it is certain that a re-evaluation of his work is in order.

All three motion pictures show pre-production planning, and it is simple to follow the story line. All have constructed sets, a considerable number of interior and exterior scenes, a good wardrobe, and a large cast. The pictures are broken up into scenes or tableaux, each preceded by a descriptive title, and there is frequent camera movement, including inserts and closeups, but only when needed to get a point across to the audience.

Lubin's cameramen had sufficient photographic knowledge of lighting to match interiors with exteriors, something that was difficult for early cameramen to accomplish with even a modicum of success, for emulsion on raw stock was unstable, and there was lack of laboratory control. Siegmund "Pop" Lubin had a very fine motion picture film developing laboratory, and his cameramen were skilled at exposing their film to obtain such photographic effects as could be added in the laboratory.

SHE WOULD BE AN ACTRESS is a lighthearted 167-foot comedy about a housewife who reads a book on "How To Become An Actress" and determines to be one. In the cast are Kempton Greene, and Leonard C. Shumway. The film was copyrighted on August 5, 1909.

She Would Be An Actress

DRUNKARD'S CHILD is a 251-foot melodrama of a little crippled newsboy who, because of an act of honesty, is adopted by a wealthy couple, over the protests of his drunken father. The copyright date is August 9, 1909.

Drunkard's Child

The third Lubin motion picture, AN UNEXPECTED GUEST, is another melodrama. The "guest" is a baby whose birth almost prevents a wedding from taking place. The whole film is built around a postscript being cut off the bottom of a letter by a father who did not wish his son to marry the woman who had written it. AN UNEXPECTED GUEST, copyrighted on August 12, 1909, was 361 feet long.

Legitimate film producers put their copyright insignia somewhere in each scene. In the early years, "Pop" Lubin had developed to a high level the ability to obliterate these insignia while duping prints. He did this by the simple expedient of inserting a matte in the printer he was using to make copies. To prevent this from happening to him, Lubin changed his copyright insigne as many as four times in a single film, placing it in a different position in each scene. Some of his copyrights were a Liberty bell, the shield of Columbia, the letters S and L intertwined so that they resembled a dollar sign, and S.L.Mfg. Co.

Siegmund Lubin retired from film-making around 1917, but remained in the optical business until his death in 1923.

An Unexpected Guest

FOOLS OF FATE

Colossal, stupendous, and gigantic are the usual adjectives used to describe Griffith's productions. But FOOLS OF FATE, his 167th picture, must have set some kind of a record for a low budget film. The only actors in it are James Kirkwood, the husband, Marion Leonard as his wife, and Frank Powell, as her paramour. There are no changes of costume in the picture. Only two sets were used, one for the dramatic scene in the paramour's cabin, and another that had been used in an AM&B moving picture before Griffith joined the studio. The balance of the film was photographed outdoors, while the company was on location at Cuddebackville, New York.

The synopsis of FOOLS OF FATE, taken from an AM&B handbill, reads, "A life story showing how foolish it is to rebel against the designs of Fate. A young woman, tired of her lot, elopes with a man, who is himself innocent of any wrong, only to find in him the person to whom her husband owes his life, he having previously saved him from drowning. The husband follows his wife and her unknown companion, and is amazed to find the unwitting wrecker of his home the man to whom he has sworn eternal friendship."

Griffith was well aware of the effect that dramatic lighting could bring to a film, and used it regularly in his pictures, including the last scene of FOOLS OF FATE.

When the discredited wife returns to her darkened cabin, the sole source of light is the lantern she holds. Then she discovers the body of her husband who has committed suicide. She drops the lantern, extinguishing it, returning the room to semi-darkness, the only light coming through the open window.

Top: Frank Powell and Marion Leonard
Bottom: Frank Powell, Marion Leonard
and James Kirkwood.

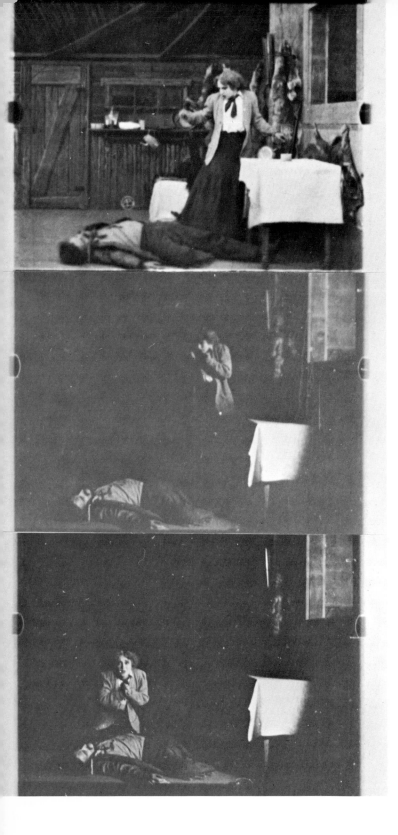

Early in his career at Biograph, Griffith learned about "effect" or "mood" lighting—perhaps even before he started to direct. A film, THE MUSIC MASTER, in which Griffith had the main role, photographed by Bitzer and released by AM&B on May 6, 1908, had a lighting effect similar to the one in FOOLS OF FATE, also photographed by Bitzer. FOOLS OF FATE seems to have been overlooked by film historians, even though it was released only three days after PIPPA PASSES, a film that invariably is mentioned because of its unusual and effective mood lighting.

FOOLS OF FATE, 363 feet long, was copyrighted on October 7, 1909, under the Biograph label. About May of 1909, AM&B decided to release their projection prints under the Biograph banner, and Mutoscope flip cards for peep shows were their only productions copyrighted under the AM&B label from that time on.

148

FAITHFUL

Not long after FOOLS OF FATE was completed, winter set in on the east coast. Rather than limit the scope of Griffith's films, which were receiving considerable acclaim, to indoor production, Biograph officials sent Griffith and a company of actors out to the continuous sunshine of California. By this time Griffith had completed over 200 films and had been a Biograph director for almost two years. His position as a writer, director, and production manager was well established. His embarrassment at being associated with motion pictures had been forgotten, and his career was well under way.

FAITHFUL, one of the films made during that first California sojourn, was quite a departure from the usual artistic, sentimental melodramas for which D. W. Griffith was becoming so well known, and quite a change of pace as well.

FAITHFUL is a comedy of feature length about an oafish character, Mack Sennett, who is struck by Arthur Johnson's chauffeur-driven automobile. The result of that encounter changes both of their lives. Mack Sennett's injuries are slight, but the efforts of the automobile owner to placate him for the damage he imagines he inflicted are so abundant that the oaf just cannot bear to let the man out of his sight. The film consists of a series of amusing incidents that show the benefactor's unsuccessful attempts to rid himself of the pest, who is enjoying the benefits of his new friendship so much he is determined it is not going to end. Everything is set right at the close of the film when the simpleton saves his benefactor's fiancee from a burning house. She had broken her engagement because of the oaf's persistence in hanging around.

Of the many parts Mack Sennett had from the time he went to work at AM&B, only the role of the simpleton in FAITHFUL seems to have been tailored to order for his talents.

Except for the scenes photographed in Biograph's new studio on Pico and Georgia Streets in Los Angeles, all of the action was shot in and around the little town of Hollywood. One scene, photographed from the summit of a hill, looks south toward Hollywood Boulevard where the Roosevelt Hotel stands today. The photography was shared between Arthur Marvin and Billy Bitzer. FAITHFUL was 408 feet long and has a copyright date of March 28, 1910.

The principal players in FAITHFUL, in addition to Mack Sennett, were Arthur Johnson and Florence Barker, but most of the cast who came to California with Griffith on that first trip had small roles in the picture, in accordance with Griffith's usual production custom.

HIS TRUST
HIS TRUST FULFILLED
ENOCH ARDEN

By 1911 the infant motion picture business was again outgrowing its playpen. American directors, eager to escape from the restrictions imposed by one reel of film, were constantly arguing with film producers. Directors wanted to make multi-reel motion pictures, but producers did not. Multi-reel European motion pictures with good entertainment value were arriving in the United States, where they gradually were winning public acceptance.

Up to this time, producers had resisted the idea of longer films on several grounds, but, no matter what reason they gave for not wanting to make motion pictures of more than one reel, there had been scant precedent among American distributors to justify increasing film budget expenditures. There was nothing to show that the return on their investment would be greater simply because the film was increased in length. And who was to say that just because motion pictures were longer that they would be better, or that audiences could be persuaded to sit through them?

Another matter that concerned film producers and theatre owners of the time was whether they could charge enough at the box office to offset the costs of longer films. The success of European imports suggested that they could. In September of 1910 statistics were released in the *New York Sun* indicating that an estimated five million persons paid to see an average of five shows a day in the 7,500 theatres throughout the United States. It is easy, therefore, to understand why theatre owners believed that five shows per day at five or ten cents were a safer bet for them than to try to get an equal amount of money out of fewer shows a day with longer films and a higher admission charge.

Contrary to the general feeling of the motion picture business, Biograph announced on June 3, 1911 in one of the better-known motion picture trade magazines the release of ENOCH ARDEN, the "first Biograph double reel," motion picture. The article also referred to two other films they had released back in January of 1911, called HIS TRUST and HIS TRUST FULFILLED. Griffith had intended them to be combined as a two-reeler, but the management thought otherwise and released them individually, one reel at a time, an action that necessitated an explanatory title preceding each reel.

The same article starts out "Announcement is made that the Biograph will soon add to the list of two-reel releases a visualization of Tennyson's poem, "Enoch Arden," each reel being complete in itself, but so planned that the two on a program offer the complete poem and this with little or no departure from the story in verse." The writer goes on to say, "The Biograph company will make no advance prediction of the success of the reel," which makes it seem that even though they announced ENOCH ARDEN as a two-reeler, they wanted theatre owners to know that it also could be purchased as separate reels, just as HIS TRUST and HIS TRUST FULFILLED had been offered some months earlier.

For HIS TRUST and HIS TRUST FULFILLED, copyrighted in January of 1911, D. W. Griffith hired an eminent writer, Emmett Campbell Hall, to do the script. The second reel begins with an explanatory title that is actually a synopsis of the first reel, "The master leaving home to join the Confederate Army, tells his body-servant to take good care of his wife and child. The master is killed in battle; the home is sacked and burned, leaving the woman and child homeless, and the old Negro, faithful to his trust, gives up his little cabin for their comfort. The only thing saved from the wreckage was the master's sword. The opening scene of the second reel takes place four years afterwards." In order to indicate the time lapse, Griffith substituted older actors in some instances, while he had others aged by makeup.

The body-servant, the principal actor in the picture, was played by Wilfred Lucas in blackface, as were all the other Negro parts in the picture. It may have been the influence of the script writer, or perhaps it was because the film covered so many years, but, for almost the first time, D. W. Griffith made use of titles to precede several scenes.

"His Trust" is the first part of a life story, the second part being "His Trust Fulfilled," and while the second is the sequel to the first, each part is a complete story in itself

The principals in the large cast were Wilfred Lucas, Claire McDowell, Del Henderson, Gladys Egan, Dorothy West, and Verner Clarges although, as usual, everybody on the Biograph lot took part in battle and crowd scenes.

HIS TRUST, 386 feet long, was copyrighted on January 19, 1911, and HIS TRUST FULFILLED, 388 feet, was copyrighted on January 24, 1911. Both were photographed in Fort Lee, New Jersey by Billy Bitzer near the end of 1910, just before the company left on its second trip to California, where Bitzer photographed ENOCH ARDEN in Santa Monica.

It is difficult to understand, in view of Biograph's opposition to two-reelers, why Griffith chose to remake one of his 1908 films, AFTER MANY YEARS, to use as a spearhead two-reeler, rather than to take a new script and a good script writer as he did with HIS TRUST FULFILLED. Instead, ENOCH ARDEN turned out to be a rather ponderous moving picture. Tennyson's poem, like many other classics, did not lend itself to a silent motion picture, and titles were necessary throughout to fill in gaps where actors could not convey the idea with gestures alone. Griffith took some license with ENOCH ARDEN; the titles were not entirely in the words of Tennyson, and he added a scene of Enoch on the desert island that was not part of the poem.

And, although ENOCH ARDEN was a two-reeler, Griffith did not depart from the camera procedure he had established for his one reel films. Once he placed the camera, all of the action was photographed, regardless of its place in the picture.

Wilfred Lucas, Frank Grandin, Linda Arvidson, Grace Henderson, Florence LaBadie, Robert Harron, Jeanie Macpherson, Alfred Paget, and George Nicholls make up the cast.

Griffith apparently was fascinated by the story line of Tennyson's poem "Enoch Arden," for not only did he use it in 1908 as the basis for the one-reel film AFTER MANY YEARS, and again in 1911 for a two-reeler called ENOCH ARDEN, but in 1915 he supervised his protege from Biograph days, Walter Christy Cabanne, when Cabanne directed a motion picture called THE FATAL MARRIAGE, still another version of the Tennyson poem. It was copyrighted as a five-reeler in 1922.

The master leaving home to join the Confederate Army, tells his body-servant to take good care of his wife and child. The master is killed in battle; the home is sacked and burned, leaving the woman and child homeless, and the old negro, faithful to his trust, gives up his little cabin for their comfort. The only thing saved from the wreckage was the master's sword.

The opening scene takes place four years afterwards

First Biograph Double Reel

Enoch Arden so Divided as to Form Two Stories Which Combine to Relate the Complete Narrative.

ANNOUNCEMENT is made that the Biograph will soon add to the list of two-reel releases a visualization of Tennyson's poem "Enoch Arden," each reel being complete in itself, but so planned that the two on a program offer the complete poem and this with little or no departure from the story as told in verse.

Not long since the Biograph released two stories, "His Trust" and "His Trust Fulfilled,"

the Biograph studios will wait with interest the release of Enoch Arden.

The first reel will deal with the love story of the seaman, his departure on a voyage and terminate with the shipwreck which leaves him a castaway on a desert island. The second reel treats with the subsequent remarriage of his wife (who believes that Enoch perished with his ship) the rescue of the castaway and his return home to discover his wife happy in her new life. His second departure from home, without hav-

A CIRCUIT AND AN INVENTION.

The Onaipa photoplay theatre, established by the Voegtle Brothers in Sharpsburg, Pa., in 1907, is the oldest house in the city and one of the oldest established in the State. It is noted for the excellence of its films and the superiority of its projection throughout that section of the country.

The theatre has been absorbed by the V. L. V. Electric Co., which has been formed by the present owners to establish a chain of theatres and boom the V. L. V. arc coil, an invention of theirs which has been in use at the Onaipa for the past two years and which has been successfully used by other Western Pennsylvania operators.

The Voegtle Brothers purpose adding five other houses to their circuit, in addition to pushing the arc coil, and have capitalized for $100,000.

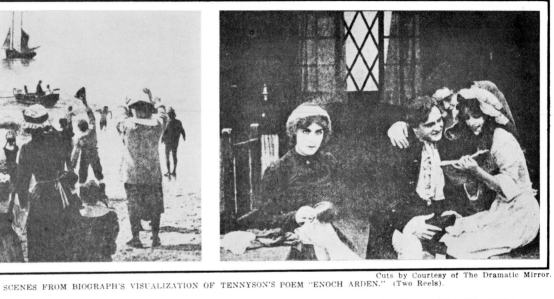

Cuts by Courtesy of The Dramatic Mirror.

SCENES FROM BIOGRAPH'S VISUALIZATION OF TENNYSON'S POEM "ENOCH ARDEN." (Two Reels).

which were connected in the sense that one was a sequel to the other, but this is the first Biograph release that properly qualifies as a two-reel production.

With their customary reticence, the Biograph Company will make no advance prediction of the success of the reel, contenting themselves with the bare announcement that such a double reel has been produced, but those familiar with "The Golden Supper" and other visualized poems from

ing disclosed his identity, more desolate than in the solitude of the lonely isle, is a strong dramatic point, but the exact handling of the climax has not been announced.

The story of Enoch Arden has furnished the suggestion for literally hundreds of stories, dramas and photoplays, but it is not evident that the original tale has been improved upon and photoplay lovers will welcome the production of the story made with the finish that is the hallmark of the circled A-B. The four cuts here reproduced will give a hint of the production and the personnel of the players.

COSTELLO AT THE ARENA.

Monday, May 22, was Vitagraph night at the Arena photoplay theatre, 172 Flatbush avenue, Brooklyn, and Maurice Costello was the star of the evening. He made a humorous speech, did some recitations and otherwise made himself solid with an audience that packed the place. There was a turning away of more than a hundred.

Following the performance Manager Rosenberg tendered him a reception at the Clarendon, where there was a fine supper and more speaking of pieces.

SCENES FROM BIOGRAPH'S VISUALIZATION OF TENNYSON'S POEM "ENOCH ARDEN."

THE GIRL AND HER TRUST

Biograph officials were not entirely convinced of the economic soundness of making multi-reel films for, even after the release of Griffith's ENOCH ARDEN in June of 1911, they continued their policy of producing only one-reel motion pictures. In the interim between June of 1911 and March of 1912, Biograph released 73 one-reel motion pictures. The 74th, THE GIRL AND HER TRUST, made by Griffith in March of 1912, is a remarkable film that appears to be a remake of a rather well-known motion picture, THE LONEDALE OPERATOR, released by Biograph one year earlier.

The paper from which THE GIRL AND HER TRUST was restored had begun to disintegrate, and the last few feet of this 369-foot motion picture are now entirely lost. Nevertheless, the film shows clearly how competent Griffith had become as a motion picture director.

THE GIRL AND HER TRUST is the story of a girl telegraph operator who works in a railroad station. She is besieged by two robbers intent on stealing a cash box entrusted to her care but is able to transmit one message for help before they cut the telegraph wire. During her battle to thwart the robbers, the girl moves back and forth between the telegraph key and the door bolt. In desperation, she thinks of a ruse to frighten them off, and pokes a cartridge into the keyhole of the door, then hits it with a hammer. So that the audience could participate in the excitement, Griffith moved his camera in for as expressive a tight closeup as he ever used in any of his films.

Despite the girl's valiant efforts, the robbers escape with the money, taking her as hostage. They used a trackmender's cart for their getaway vehicle. Griffith used a train preceding the getaway cart down the railroad track as a camera platform.

This motion picture also contains one of the best examples of Griffith's use of the cutback. In the chase sequence, he frequently changes the scene from the robbers fleeing with the girl and the money to the engine on which the pursuing rescuers are riding, each time shortening the interval between cutbacks, until the actual capture.

Throughout the picture, Griffith made liberal use of camera movement, cutbacks, inserts, and closeups, and, in one scene, to establish point of view between two persons as well as to indicate their next action, Griffith panned back and forth between the villains and the station master. It is the sole example of such camera use by Griffith in the Biograph films restored from paper.

The copyright date of THE GIRL AND HER TRUST is March 28, 1912, and it was photographed in California. In the cast are Dorothy Bernard, Wilfred Lucas, Alfred Paget, Charles Gorman, Charles West, Charles Hill Mailes, Tony O'Sullivan, and Robert Harron.

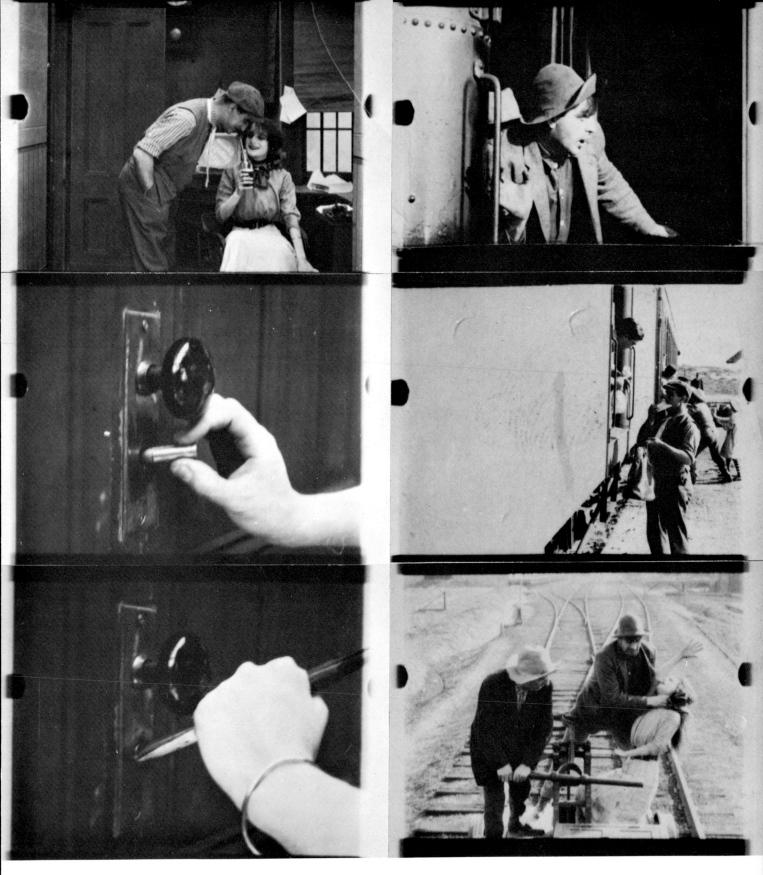

Scenes from THE GIRL AND HER TRUST

THE AVIATOR'S GENEROSITY
LOVE AND FRIENDSHIP

Multi-reel motion pictures were being made in Europe before Biograph began experimenting with two-reel films. A Danish film producer, the Nordisk Film Company, had been successfully making and releasing two and three reel films since 1910 as a matter of course. Paper copies of 16 different titles produced by this company in 1911 and 1912 were deposited in the Library of Congress archives and later restored. Every one of the 16 is at least two full reels, while some are longer.

Nordisk began producing motion pictures around 1906 and, by 1910 had one of the largest and best-equipped studios anywhere on the Continent, or in the world, for that matter, employing over 500 craftsmen. Their films were distributed mainly in the Scandinavian countries, Germany, and Russia.

In 1908 Nordisk Film Company appointed Ingvald C. Oes, American-born graduate of the Royal Industrial Art School in Oslo, Norway, as their American representative, and he opened an office in New York, just a few doors east of AM&B's studio on Fourteenth Street. The Nordisk Film Company was known in America as the Great Northern Film Company, and had as its trademark a polar bear sitting on top of the world.

Little is known of Oes's activities when he returned to America to establish himself as a film distributor. It is known, however, that Oes went along with the independent film producers, rather than with the patent combine, or trust. This may be one answer to why the films made by Nordisk were copyrighted in his name in the United States — a protective measure. The legal battle between the trust and the independent film-makers and distributors was in its last throes when Oes decided to join the independents, perhaps an error in judgment, because no record could be found that these 16 films were ever shown in this country. Whatever the reason, they remained unknown until they were restored from paper copies. The Danish Film Museum has been able to supply the names of directors, cast, and some production details.

Ole Olson, owner and supervisor of all Nordisk films, felt that motion pictures showing how the small group of rich and aristocratic people lived would appeal to the larger group of ticket-buyers, so all productions were on a lavish scale. Nordisk's films are professionally made, even by today's standards. All sets are architecturally well constructed. The art direction reflects good taste in the selection of costumes, props, and buildings used as backgrounds. Props are placed to allow actors freedom of action, and the films show a great deal of pre-production planning. There is ample camera movement to bring the audience into the filmed story, as well as to add to its clarity, and the photography indicates that their cameramen were well versed in their craft. Usual light source for interiors was the sun diffused through the glass roofs of Nordisk's five studios.

Modern film-makers have sound to aid them in telling a story, but these films, of course, are silent, and the actors are Scandinavian, with gestures of communication entirely different from those of American or British actors. Nevertheless, the stories depicted in these films hold the interest of the audience and are easily followed, with remarkably few titles. All of their performers were graduates of Denmark's Royal Academy or were highly skilled professionals from other countries. Not so in America and Britain where producers commonly recruited members of their families to serve as actors in their motion pictures.

THE AVIATOR'S GENEROSITY

Christian Nobel, who wrote the script for this 821-foot motion picture, took his inspiration from the newest, most exciting invention of the century, the airplane. The plot involves two aviators, the sister of one, and an airplane race. A plane used in the film was built by a Danish engineer, while another was a French Bleriot.

THE AVIATOR'S GENEROSITY was directed by August Blom, a former stage director, and Christel Holck, Poul Reumert, and Einar Zangenberg are the principals. The film was copyrighted in the United States by Ingvald C. Oes on April 10, 1912, but it was produced in Denmark on June 1, 1911.

Top, left to right:
Christel Holck
and Einar Zangenberg

Bottom, left to right:
Christel Holck, Poul
Reumert, and
Einar Zangenberg in
AVIATOR'S
GENEROSITY

LOVE AND FRIENDSHIP

Another Nordisk film from the group of 16 restored from paper rolls is a melodrama called LOVE AND FRIEND-SHIP. This motion picture begins by showing the two principal actresses as teenagers in a boarding school. It follows their separate lives, one as a wife, the other as a singer, and then brings them together again as adults. There is a dramatic ending to the motion picture as the two women fight a duel with fencing swords over the affections of the army officer/ fencing master husband of one. The large cast includes Clara Wieth as the wife, Aage Fønss as her husband, and Agneta Blom as the singer. The 932-foot film was copyrighted in the United States by Ingvald C. Oes on April 24, 1912. Date of production in Denmark was September 27, 1911.

LOVE AND FRIENDSHIP: Top, left to right, Aage Fønss, Agneta Blom, and Clara Wieth. Bottom: Agneta Blom and Clara Wieth.

A TEMPORARY TRUCE

Although much ado was made about the release of Griffith's two-reel motion picture, ENOCH ARDEN, a year of production went by before another film of such magnitude was undertaken at Biograph, when Griffith made the two-reel A TEMPORARY TRUCE. A unique story, superb camera movement, and the large cast for 1912, all combine to make a A TEMPORARY TRUCE a milestone for Biograph as producer, as well as for D. W. Griffith as film director. It is a mystery why this motion picture was overlooked by the contemporary press, as it has been by film historians for the last half century. When we interviewed one of the principals, the late Claire McDowell, she had no recollection of ever making it, nor did the lead, Blanche Sweet.

A TEMPORARY TRUCE was photographed in California by Billy Bitzer. The film is about two men who are determined to kill one another, and who are forced to declare a temporary truce in order to fight a common enemy and save themselves and the woman about whom they are quarreling. Their common enemy is a tribe of Indians, set on the warpath by some irresponsible cowboys, who without purpose or reason, kill one of the tribe's elders.

The battle between the Indians and the principals was photographed from many positions, the first from the top of a hill that overlooked the woman and the two men in the valley completely surrounded by Indians intent on revenge. As they began to converge, Griffith moved his camera to the position occupied by the principals to show, from their point of view, the danger from the gradually narrowing circle of Indians. Griffith emphasized the battle, gave his scenes more power, and built up suspense by improving on a device he had employed in his second month as a director of having the Indians proceed toward the camera from a distance, thereby lengthening the scene. As each Indian neared the camera, Griffith cut to one of the principals firing a gun, then quickly cut back to the Indian, photographing him as he fell. After moving the camera a number of times to record the firing on both sides, Griffith returned the camera to the position of his establishing shot to show the circle of dead Indians in the valley below, and that the townspeople had arrived to help their friends.

A TEMPORARY TRUCE was copyrighted by Biograph on June 10, 1912 and was 570 feet long. The cast consists of Blanche Sweet, Claire McDowell, Charles West, Walter Chrystie Miller, Alfred Paget, Walter Christy Cabanne, Robert Harron, Charles Hill Mailes and Charles Gorman.

A Temporary Truce

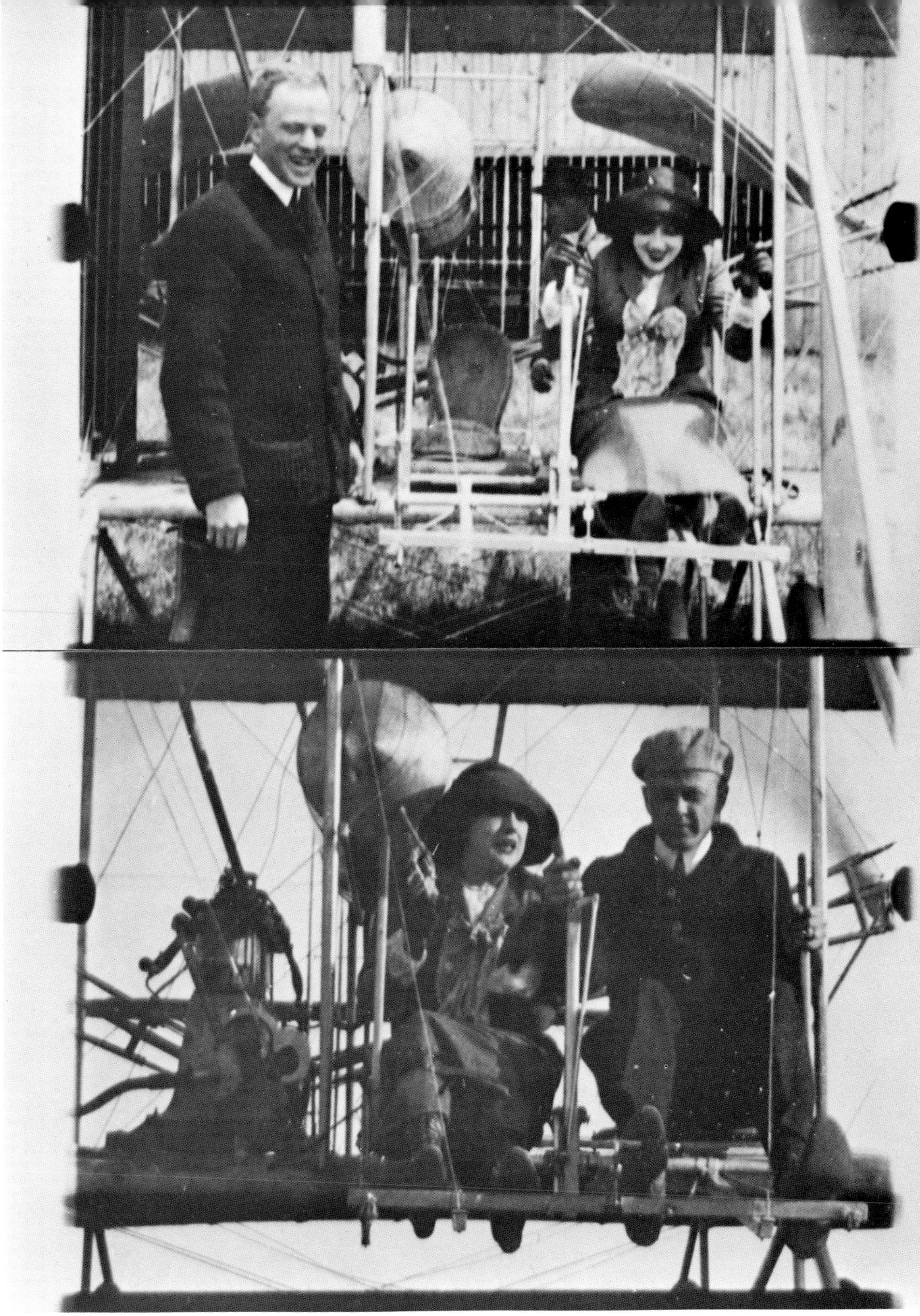

*Mabel
Normand
and
Philip
Parmalee*

A DASH THROUGH THE CLOUDS

At the end of December 1913 a curious ad four columns wide that had already appeared in several trade magazines was reprinted in the *New York Dramatic Mirror* announcing to the world D. W. Griffith's achievements and contributions to the motion picture business. It was signed by Albert H. T. Banzhaf, who styled himself "Counsellor-at-Law" and "Personal Representative." Banzhaf certified that, "For two years from the Summer of 1908, Mr. Griffith personally directed all Biograph motion pictures. Thereafter as general director he superintended all Biograph productions and directed the more *important* features until October 1, 1913."

The ad also contained a list that proved to be incomplete of over 150 films that Griffith had personally directed. Not listed, but among those he "superintended" was a short comedy called A DASH THROUGH THE CLOUDS that is a good example of how so many motion pictures were made in the early years, on the spur of the moment, with little thought to story. After all, the company had had several years of experience with a format that was successful with audiences and film distributors — the chase. All that was needed to make one film different from another was a gimmick.

In this particular film, it was Philip Parmalee and his airplane. Parmalee was a member of the first group of aviators taught by Wilbur Wright. A DASH THROUGH THE CLOUDS was a split-reel comedy directed by Mack Sennett, who gained much of his initial experience as a director with this kind of motion picture.

The format of A DASH THROUGH THE CLOUDS was a standard chase except that Sennett employed an airplane to chase the errant husband who was escaping on horseback. A device of Griffith's for stretching out a scene and sustaining suspense was to position a camera and make his subjects come toward it from a great distance. Mack Sennett adopted this same method for A DASH THROUGH THE CLOUDS. He placed the camera on a hilltop and directed the airplane to fly over the camera from several different directions. This accomplished two things: it changed the background, and, when the scenes were edited together, gave the audience the impression that the airplane actually was pursuing the man on horseback. In some scenes, to make the audience believe that a camera was in the airplane while it was flying, the plane was placed on supports on the ground in such a way that the horizon was invisible. Parmalee and Normand were directed to act as though the plane really was aloft.

The comedy also gave Sennett an opportunity of offering the movie-going public the somewhat unusual sight for that day of a woman in an airplane. Part of the copy under Mabel Normand's picture in WHO'S WHO IN THE FILM WORLD, published two years later, reads, "Miss Normand bears the distinction of being the first girl ever to fly in an aeroplane with the late Philip Parmalee."

Left to Right: Jack Pickford, Kate Bruce, Alfred Paget, Sylvia Ashton, and Fred Mace in A DASH THROUGH THE CLOUDS.

A DASH THROUGH THE CLOUDS was photographed in Culver City, California, during Biograph's second winter on the west coast. In addition to Mabel Normand and Philip Parmalee, the cast consisted of Fred Mace, Kate Bruce, Sylvia Ashton, Jack Pickford, and Alfred Paget, some of whom joined Mack Sennett as salaried employees of the Keystone Film Company. Copyright date of the film is June 28, 1912.

The Banzhaf/Griffith advertisement of 1913, after listing the films that Griffith had directed, concluded "Also two, three, and four-reel features not yet released for exhibition in America, including JUDITH OF BETHULIA, THE MASSACRE, THE BATTLE *OF* ELDERBUSH GULCH, and WARS OF THE PRIMAL TRIBES."

Much has been written about the termination of Griffith's association with Biograph, how it happened, and what caused it. This is not an attempt to add or subtract from anything already in print but simply to correlate some dates, add some production information, and to clear up some confusion as to film titles, for whatever value that information may have.

Take the first of the aforementioned unreleased Griffith films, JUDITH OF BETHULIA. There are two copyrights connected with this picture, October 31, 1913, and November 17, 1913, but it wasn't until a year later that this four-reel motion picture was made available to exhibitors, for release one reel at a time. JUDITH OF BETHULIA is a religious motion picture that involved more persons, more time, and more money, and was longer than any picture Griffith had made up to that time for Biograph, yet in this instance Biograph didn't follow its usual exploitation policy of releasing a motion picture as soon as it was completed and had been copyrighted.

THE MASSACRE, the second of the four films listed as not yet released in the Banzhaf/Griffith ad, was described as follows in a June 1912 issue of THE MOVING PICTURE WORLD:

"An interesting situation which is now developing will be presented within the next two months when two of the big manufacturers will release, at about the same time, big special productions of the same subject. The Biograph Company and the Bison Company have just produced pictures dealing with the Custer massacre and the events leading up to it. The Bison's production will be another big three-reel effort of the kind which is rapidly making that company's lasting fame. The Biograph's production of the same subject will make two reels, according to report. An interesting fact is that both pictures were made within ten or fifteen miles of each other and both were finished on the same day and the negatives were probably carried East on the same train. The Biograph's picture was produced at San Fernando . . . . The secrecy which usually surrounds the making of Biograph pictures was in this case broken down by the magnitude of the production."

The production was so large that the little town of San Fernando closed all business and moved out to watch D. W. Griffith direct the big scene. When the Griffith film reached New York, the Biograph officials apparently did not share the opinion of the reporter for THE MOVING PICTURE WORLD who was sure that Biograph would release "the big special production" within two months, for they still had not released THE MASSACRE when the Banzhaf/Griffith list appeared late in 1913, although the picture had been copyrighted on September 20, 1912, more than a year before.

The story of THE MASSACRE is of a young couple making their way west with a wagon train that is attacked by Indians. From that point on, the story does very little but give Griffith an opportunity for many camera positions and long shots, as well as closeups of the action when the cavalry joins the fight.

The cast of THE MASSACRE consists of Wilfred Lucas, Charles West, Blanche Sweet, Eddie Dillon, Claire McDowell, Charles Hill Mailes, Alfred Paget, Del Henderson, Walter Chrystie Miller, Charles Craig, and Robert Harron. This is another film for which D. W. Griffith is credited as having written the script.

About one year and close to 100 one-reel motion pictures later, Mr. Griffith was back in the same California valley with more Indians, more horses, and about the same principal actors in his cast, shooting another western. This time it was a superb film titled THE BATTLE *AT* ELDERBUSH GULCH, the third unreleased picture mentioned in the ad. This film was copyrighted twice in July of 1913 as THE BATTLE *AT* ELDERBUSH GULCH, although it turns up fairly often in print as THE BATTLE *AT OR OF* ELDER-*BERRY* GULCH.

Mae Marsh, Lillian Gish, Robert Harron, Kate Bruce, and Henry B. Walthall are among the cast. The copyright dates are July 1 and 15, 1913.

WARS OF THE PRIMAL TRIBES was the last of four film titles certified by Mr. Banzhaf as motion pictures made by D. W. Griffith that were still to be released. That unknown title started some research that brought to light the following facts. WARS OF THE PRIMAL TRIBES did not reach the screen or the Copyright Office by that name, but rolls of paper from an original negative of a three-reel motion picture called THE PRIMITIVE MAN were sent by Biograph to the Copyright Office on November 14 and 24, 1913.

Back in the summer of 1912, Griffith wrote the script for and directed a one-reel film called MAN'S GENESIS. He considered it a contribution to serious motion picture drama because of its subject, the then-controversial theory of man's evolution, and perhaps the best work he had ever done. But L. E. Dougherty, Biograph's scenario editor and production head, did not agree with Griffith and felt that it should be released as a comedy. A battle resulted. Mr. Dougherty apparently had the last word, since the film was described as a comedy by Biograph when they released it in July of 1912.

MAN'S GENESIS is Griffith's conjecture of how primitive man lived and survived, climaxed by a fight between two primitive males (Robert Harron as "Weakhands" and Wilfred Lucas as "Brute Force") over a female (Mae Marsh as "Lilywhite"). Brains win out over brawn as the husky man loses to the weak man, who uses a weapon he had just invented for his defense. The actors all wear costumes fashioned from animal skins or grasses, and make their homes in caves.

In addition to the above members of the cast, Walter Chrystie Miller, and a number of others who cannot be identified because of their makeup, are in the 414-foot picture.

As previously mentioned, a year and a half after the release of MAN'S GENESIS, Biograph copyrighted a three-reel motion picture called THE PRIMITIVE MAN, also written by Griffith, released in England in March 1914, and in this country as BRUTE FORCE in April 1914. When the films made from the paper rolls of MAN'S GENESIS and THE PRIMITIVE MAN were compared, it was discovered that PRIMITIVE MAN is almost identical in story with MAN'S GENESIS, except that it is two reels longer, or 1,170 feet.

Griffith devoted the first reel of his three-reel version to scenes of a young man who falls asleep at his club while reading a book by Darwin on the theory of man's evolution and then has a dream about it. The second and third reels follow the story line of MAN'S GENESIS.

MAN'S GENESIS was photographed entirely outside, while THE PRIMITIVE MAN had some rather elaborate and expensive sets, a much larger cast, as well as some live animals and reptiles disguised by the addition of false wings, tails, and horns to make them appear as prehistoric monsters. There is even a photograph of a moving set, at least 40 feet high, that is constructed to resemble a dinosaur.

Griffith used the same three principals, Mae Marsh, Robert Harron, and Wilfred Lucas, for the roles of Lilywhite, Weakhands, and Brute Force, as he had used in MAN'S GENESIS. Also in the cast was Alfred Paget, Edwin August, Charles Hill Mailes, and William J. Butler.

Applications for copyright for over 6,000 individual moving pictures were sent to the Library of Congress between 1894 and 1913. From the approximately 3,000 that remained and were restored from paper rolls to motion pictures, it is possible to learn much about the beginnings of an industry and an art form that by 1914 had reached its voting age. Experience and precedence now made it possible to decide what type of films to make that would be successful at the box office. With the advent of mobility of motion picture equipment that gave the director more opportunity to take his audience with him, and improved lighting to show the way, he started all over again in 1914 remaking, only bigger, better, and more magnificent, all of the films that had been made in the previous ten years.

INDEXES

FILM TITLES IN ALPHABETICAL ORDER

FILM TITLES IN ALPHABETICAL ORDER

FILM TITLES IN ALPHABETICAL ORDER

FILM TITLES IN CHRONOLOGICAL ORDER

FILM TITLE	PRODUCER	COPYRIGHT DATE
Edison Kinetoscopic Record of A Sneeze	Edison	Jan. 9, 1894
Black Diamond Express	Edison	Dec. 12, 1896
Parisian Dance	Edison	Jan. 15, 1897
Corbett—Fitzsimmons Fight	Lubin	not copyrighted
Elopement on Horseback	Edison	Nov. 26, 1898
Passion Play, The	Hollaman	not copyrighted
Strange Adventure of New York Drummer	Edison	June 17, 1899
Trip To The Moon, A	Lubin	June 26, 1899
Love and War	J. H. White	Nov. 28, 1899
Cinderella	Melies	not copyrighted
Dreyfus Court Martial	Melies	not copyrighted
Paris Exposition	Melies	not copyrighted
Uncle Josh's Nightmare	Edison	Mar. 21, 1900
Terrible Teddy, The Grizzly King	Edison	Feb. 23, 1901
Love By The Light Of The Moon	Edison	Mar. 16, 1901
Circular Panorama of Electric Tower	Edison	Aug. 14, 1901
Martyred Presidents	Edison	Oct. 7, 1901
Panorama of Esplanade by Night	Edison	Nov. 11, 1901
Country Couple	Edison	not copyrighted
Uncle Josh at the Moving Picture Show	Edison	Jan. 27, 1902
Twentieth Century Tramp, The	Edison	Jan. 27, 1902
Fun In A Bakery Shop	Edison	Apr. 3, 1902
Jack and the Beanstalk	Edison	June 20, 1902
Grandpa's Reading Glass	AM&B	Oct. 3, 1902
Life of An American Fireman	Edison	Jan. 21, 1903
Uncle Tom's Cabin	Lubin	May 1, 1903
Tom, Tom, the Piper's Son	Lubin	May 1, 1903
Inn Where No Man Rests, The	Melies	June 25, 1903
Spiritualist Photographer, A	Melies	July 6, 1903
Uncle Tom's Cabin	Edison	July 30, 1903
Search For Evidence, A	AM&B	Aug. 3, 1903
Gay Shoe Clerk	Edison	Aug. 12, 1903
Dude and the Burglars, The	AM&B	Aug. 13, 1903
Kingdom of the Fairies, The	Melies	Sept. 3, 1903
Trip to the Moon, A	Melies	not copyrighted
Romance of the Rail, A	Edison	Oct. 3, 1903
Great Train Robbery, The	Edison	Dec. 1, 1903
Magic Lantern, The	Melies	Dec. 9, 1903
Pickpocket, The	Gaumont	Dec. 10, 1903
How The Old Woman Caught The Omnibus	Hepworth	Dec. 19, 1903
Story the Biograph Told, The	AM&B	Jan. 8, 1904
Escaped Lunatic, The	AM&B	Jan. 12, 1904
Clock Maker's Dream, The	Melies	Feb. 23, 1904
Battle of the Yalu, The	AM&B	Mar. 23 & 29, 1904
Cook In Trouble, The	Melies	May 9, 1904
Mermaid, The	Melies	May 18, 1904
Child Stealers, The	Gaumont	June 9, 1904
Raid On A Coiner's Den	Gaumont	June 23, 1904
Eviction, The	Gaumont	June 23, 1904
Great Train Robbery	Lubin	June 27, 1904
Personal	AM&B	June 29, 1904

FILM TITLE	PRODUCER	COPYRIGHT DATE
Bold Bank Robbery	Lubin	July 25, 1904
Bewitched Traveller, The	Hepworth	Aug. 12, 1904
Moonshiner, The	AM&B	Aug. 19, 1904
How A French Nobleman Got A Wife Through The New York Herald Personal Columns	Edison	Aug. 26, 1904
Trip to Paris, A	Hepworth	not copyrighted
European Rest Cure	Edison	Sept. 1, 1904
Widow and the Only Man, The	AM&B	Sept. 8, 1904
Rounding Up of the "Yeggmen"	Edison	Sept. 16, 1904
Hero of Liao Yang, The	AM&B	Sept. 22, 1904
Revenge!	Gaumont	Oct. 1, 1904
Maniac Chase	Edison	Oct. 7, 1904
Railway Tragedy, A	Gaumont	Oct. 10, 1904
Parsifal	Edison	Oct. 13, 1904
Lost Child, The	AM&B	Oct. 15, 1904
Englishman's Trip to Paris from London, An	Clarendon, Gaumont or Hepworth	Oct. 28, 1904
Decoyed	ditto	Oct. 28, 1904
New Version of "Personal"	Lubin	Nov. 5, 1904
Suburbanite, The	AM&B	Nov. 11, 1904
Ex-Convict, The	Edison	Nov. 19, 1904
Other Side of the Hedge, The	Hepworth	Nov. 28, 1904
Race For A Kiss, A	Hepworth	Nov. 28, 1904
Lover's Ruse, The	Hepworth	Nov. 28, 1904
Kleptomaniac, The	Edison	Feb. 4, 1905
Seven Ages, The	Edison	Feb. 27, 1905
Tom, Tom, the Piper's Son	AM&B	Mar. 9, 1905
How Jones Lost His Roll	Edison	Mar. 27, 1905
Nihilists, The	AM&B	Mar. 28, 1905
Whole Dam Family and the Dam Dog	Edison	May 31, 1905
Rescued by Rover	Hepworth	Aug. 19, 1905
Fine Feathers Make Fine Birds	Unknown	Aug. 25, 1905
Great Jewel Mystery, The	AM&B	Oct. 23, 1905
Kentucky Feud, A	AM&B	Nov. 7, 1905
Dream of a Rarebit Fiend	Edison	Feb. 24, 1906
Silver Wedding, The	AM&B	Mar. 8, 1906
Black Hand, The	AM&B	Mar. 24, 1906
Paymaster, The	AM&B	June 23, 1906
Tunnel Workers, The	AM&B	Nov. 10, 1906
Skyscrapers, The	AM&B	Dec. 11, 1906
Mr. Hurry-up of New York	AM&B	Jan. 31, 1907
Girl From Montana, The	Selig	Mar. 14, 1907
His First Ride	Selig	Mar. 29, 1907
Bandit King, The	Selig	Apr. 11, 1907
Tired Tailor's Dream, The	AM&B	Aug. 27, 1907
Arcadian Elopement, An	AM&B	Sept. 16, 1907
Princess In The Vase, The	AM&B	Feb. 25, 1908
Boy Detective, The	AM&B	Mar. 7, 1908
Her First Adventure	AM&B	Mar. 13, 1908
Caught By Wireless	AM&B	Mar. 18, 1908
Sculptor's Nightmare, The	AM&B	May 4, 1908
Music Master, The	AM&B	May 6, 1908
At The French Ball	AM&B	June 20, 1908
Over The Hills To The Poorhouse	AM&B	June 20, 1908
Adventures of Dollie	AM&B	July 10, 1908

FILM TITLE	PRODUCER	COPYRIGHT DATE
Calamitous Elopement, A	AM&B	July 28, 1908
Balked At The Altar	AM&B	Aug. 15, 1908
Where Breakers Roar	AM&B	Sept. 15, 1908
After Many Years	AM&B	Oct 28, 1908
Awful Moment, An	AM&B	Dec. 10, 1908
Bank Robbery, The	Oklahoma Natural Mutoscene	Dec. 28, 1908
Round-Up In Oklahoma, A	ditto	Dec. 28, 1908
Wolf Hunt, The	ditto	Dec. 28, 1908
Cord of Life, The	AM&B	Jan. 22, 1909
Girls and Daddy, The	AM&B	Feb. 3, 1909
Golden Louis	AM&B	Feb. 17, 1909
At The Altar	AM&B	Feb. 26, 1909
She Would Be An Actress	Lubin	Aug. 5, 1909
Drunkard's Child	Lubin	Aug. 9, 1909
Unexpected Guest, An	Lubin	Aug. 12, 1909
Pippa Passes	Biograph	Oct. 4, 1909
Fools of Fate	Biograph	Oct. 7, 1909
Faithful	Biograph	Mar. 28, 1910
His Trust	Biograph	Jan. 19, 1911
His Trust Fulfilled	Biograph	Jan. 24, 1911
Lonedale Operator, The	Biograph	Mar. 25, 1911
Enoch Arden	Biograph	June 13 & 17, 1911
Girl and Her Trust, The	Biograph	Mar. 28, 1912
Coming of Columbus, The	Selig	Apr. 8, 1912
Aviator's Generosity, The	Nordisk (Oes)	Apr. 10, 1912
Love and Friendship	Nordisk (Oes)	Apr. 24, 1912
Temporary Truce, A	Biograph	June 10, 1912
Dash Through The Clouds, A	Biograph	June 28, 1912
Man's Genesis	Biograph	July 23, 1912
Massacre, The	Biograph	Sept. 20, 1912 & Oct. 30, 1912
Battle At Elderbush Gulch, The	Biograph	July 1 & 15, 1913
Judith of Bethulia	Biograph	Oct. 31, 1913 & Nov. 17, 1913
Wars Of The Primal Tribes	Biograph	not copyrighted
Primitive Man, The	Biograph	Nov. 14 & 24, 1913
Brute Force	Biograph	not copyrighted
Beating Back	Beating Back Film Corp.	not copyrighted
When Outlaws Meet	unknown	not copyrighted
Lady of The Dugout, The	unknown	not copyrighted
Fatal Marriage, The	Art Brand Productions	June 18, 1922

THE FIRST TWENTY YEARS

This book, THE FIRST TWENTY YEARS, was written with the intention of discussing the progress of filmmaking, beginning with the truly primitive short motion pictures and continuing through the introduction of multi-reel films. For that reason the motion pictures are described in order of copyright date, regardless of maker or country of origin.

But the film collection, also known as THE FIRST TWENTY YEARS, has now been assembled on reels, this time in a different order from that used in the book. The reels are arranged by maker and/or country of origin.

For your convenience, we list each of the titles on the 26 reels that make up THE FIRST TWENTY YEARS, together with the page in the book of the same name that provides the history and other details of interest about the film.

The films in THE FIRST TWENTY YEARS collection are available from Pyramid Films, Box 1048, Santa Monica, California 90406.

PYRAMID CODE # & RUNNING TIME	TITLES ON REEL	BOOK PAGE #
	EDISON/PORTER	
5001 Part I 22 minutes	Elopement On Horseback	8
	Strange Adventure of New York Drummer	8,9,19,13
	Uncle Josh's Nightmare	13
	Terrible Teddy, The Grizzly King	17
	Love By The Light Of The Moon	18
	Circular Panorama of Electric Tower	19
	Panorama of Esplanade By Night	19,20
	Martyred Presidents	21
	Uncle Josh At The Moving Picture Show	22
	The Twentieth Century Tramp	24
	Fun In A Bakery Shop	25,124
	Jack And The Beanstalk	26-28,34,82
	Life Of An American Fireman	22,30,118
	EDISON/PORTER	
5002 Part II 29 minutes	Uncle Tom's Cabin	33,34,61
	Gay Shoe Clerk	36,37
	A Romance Of The Rail	41,42
	Rounding Up Of The "Yeggmen"	68
	EDISON/PORTER — 1904 and 1905	
5003 Part III 29 minutes	European Rest Cure	66
	The Ex-Convict	82,85
	The Kleptomaniac	21,82,85,86
	EDISON/PORTER — 1905	
5004 Part IV 17 minutes	The Seven Ages	87,90
	How Jones Lost His Roll	90,92
	The Whole Dam Family And The Dam Dog	92

PYRAMID CODE # & RUNNING TIME	TITLES ON REEL	BOOK PAGE #

COMEDIES-AMERICAN MUTOSCOPE & BIOGRAPH

5005 Part V 25 minutes	The Dude And The Burglars	36,37
	The Story Of The Biograph Told	49,50,81
	Personal	57,58,60,61,77
	The Widow And The Only Man	67,68,92
	The Lost Child	77

COMEDIES-AMERICAN MUTOSCOPE & BIOGRAPH

5006 Part VI 25 minutes	The Suburbanite	80
	Tom, Tom, The Piper's Son	61,88,89
	An Acadian Elopement	116

COMEDIES-AMERICAN MUTOSCOPE & BIOGRAPH

5007 Part VII 23 minutes	Grandpa's Reading Glass	29,34
	Mr. Hurry-Up Of New York	111,112
	The Tired Tailor's Dream	111,112
	The Sculptor's Nightmare	123-125

DRAMAS-AMERICAN MUTOSCOPE & BIOGRAPH

5008 Part VIII 29 minutes	A Search For Evidence	35
	The Moonshiner	64,101
	The Hero Of Liao Yang	69,70

DRAMAS-AMERICAN MUTOSCOPE & BIOGRAPH

5009 Part IX 26 minutes	The Nihilists	91
	The Great Jewel Mystery	97,98,126
	A Kentucky Feud	100,101

DRAMAS-AMERICAN MUTOSCOPE & BIOGRAPH

5010 Part X 23 minutes	The Silver Wedding	102,103,107
	The Black Hand	103,104
	The Paymaster	105,106

DRAMAS-AMERICAN MUTOSCOPE & BIOGRAPH

5011 Part XI 18 minutes	The Tunnel Workers	107,108
	The Skyscrapers	107

AMERICAN MUTOSCOPE & BIOGRAPH

5012 Part XII
26 minutes

The Boy Detective	117
Her First Adventure	118,119
Caught By Wireless	120,121
At The French Ball	126

COMEDIES-AMERICAN MUTOSCOPE & BIOGRAPH

5013 Part XIII
27 minutes

Balked At The Altar	129,130
Faithful	149
A Dash Through The Clouds	161-163

DRAMAS-AMERICAN MUTOSCOPE & BIOGRAPH

5014 Part XIV
30 minutes

A Calamitous Elopement	128
Where Breakers Roar	131,132,137
An Awful Moment	133,137
The Cord Of Life	137-139

GRIFFITH/AMERICAN MUTOSCOPE & BIOGRAPH

5015 Part XV
23 minutes

The Girls And Daddy	139,140

GRIFFITH/AMERICAN MUTOSCOPE & BIOGRAPH

5016 Part XVI
26 minutes

The Golden Louis	141,142
At The Altar	142,143
Fools Of Fate	147,149

GRIFFITH/AMERICAN MUTOSCOPE & BIOGRAPH

5017 Part XVII
22 minutes

His Trust and His Trust Fulfilled	150-152

GRIFFITH/AMERICAN MUTOSCOPE & BIOGRAPH

5018 Part XVIII
25 minutes

Enoch Arden	150-151, 153, 154, 159

GRIFFITH/AMERICAN MUTOSCOPE & BIOGRAPH

5019 Part XIX
27 minutes

The Girl And Her Trust	154,155
A Temporary Truce	159,160

PYRAMID CODE # & RUNNING TIME	TITLES ON REEL	BOOK PAGE #
	LUBIN	
5020 Part XX 28 minutes	Bold Bank Robbery	61,62
	She Would Be An Actress	144,145
	The Drunkard's Child	144,146
	An Unexpected Guest	144,146
	EXTRAORDINARY AMERICAN FILMS	
5021 Part XXI 30 minutes	Love And War/James H. White	8,11
	The Girl From Montana/Selig	113
	His First Ride/Selig	113,114
	The Bandit King/Selig	113,114
	The Bank Robbery/Okla. Natural Mutoscene	134,135
	MELIES MOTION PICTURES	
5022 Part XXII 29 minutes	The Inn Where No Man Rests	31,32,43
	A Spiritualist Photographer	32,43
	The Kingdom Of The Fairies	38,39,43
	The Magic Lantern	43
	The Clock Maker's Dream	51
	The Cook In Trouble	52
	The Mermaid	53
	BRITISH COMEDIES	
5023 Part XXIII 22 minutes	How The Old Woman Caught The Omnibus	46,48
	The Eviction	55,56
	The Bewitched Traveller	63,64
	An Englishman's Trip To Paris From London	78,79
	The Lover's Ruse	84
	A Race For A Kiss	83
	The Other Side Of The Hedge	84
	Fine Feathers Make Fine Birds	95
	BRITISH DRAMAS	
5024 Part XXIV 30 minutes	The Pickpocket	46
	The Child Stealers	54
	Raid On A Coiner's Den	55,56
	Revenge!	71
	A Railway Tragedy	71,72
	Decoyed	79
	Rescued By Rover	93,94,119
	DANISH FILMS	
5025 Part XXV 23 minutes	The Aviator's Generosity	156,157
	DANISH FILMS	
5026 Part XXVI 26 minutes	Love And Friendship	156,158

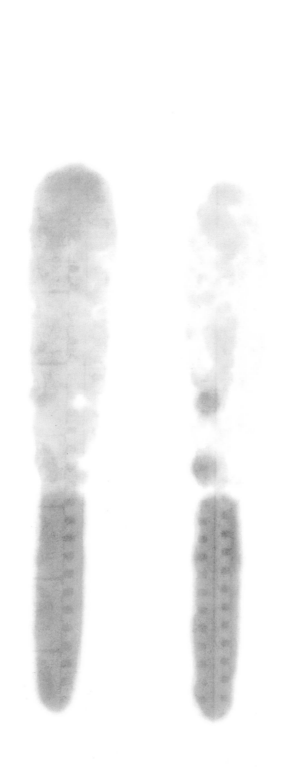

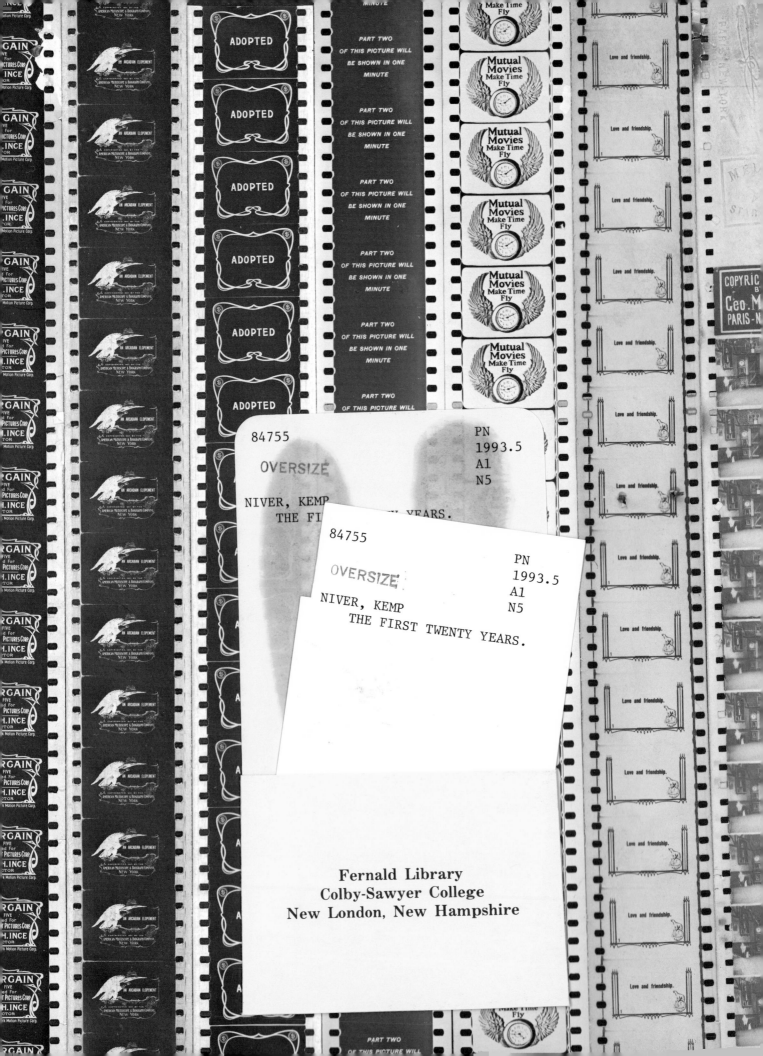